Preface

Maths Cloud Ltd was founded by a number of Maths teachers with a
resources and content to support and aid teachers in teaching Math
and across the world.

The team initially developed an online teaching platform which was launched in 2015. This
has received great reviews and feedback from teachers.

It has seen significant growth and usage since it's launch and is now used across the UK and
internationally.

Due to repeated requests from students wishing for supportive documents and resources to
our teaching platform, we launched maths-school, which is a suite of content to support
students outside the classroom.

This maths-school skills workbook, and our other workbooks, have been specifically
designed and developed to support students in practising the skills taught within the
classroom.

All our skills workbooks include examples, exam style questions and a complete set of
answers.

We continue to work hard to develop and enhance our offering, so please ensure that you
follow us on Facebook and take advantage of our detailed explanations of the topics on our
website Maths-School.co.uk

This is the 2nd workbook in a series of 3 workbooks aimed towards iGCSE. We strongly
recommend that you have completed our 1st workbook (Grades 1 to 3) before starting this
book.

Contents

Contents

Contents

Using a calculator

Both iGCSE exams include using your calculator, so you must familiarise yourself with the calculator you have. A scientific calculator is an essential item and you should become familiar with the following functions as a minimum.

The shift or 2ⁿᵈ Function button allows you to use the functions which are written above each button.

In iGCSE – ensure you are always working with degrees when it involves an angles . (It should say D at the top).

This button allow you to input fractions into your calculations.

These buttons allow you to input indices and roots into your calculations.

The S-D button on a Casio allows you to change your answer from a fraction or surd to a decimal.

The sin, cos and tan functions are essential when undertaking trigonometry.

The shift button followed by this button allows you to input π into your calculations.
(used for circles)

The Ans button will display your last calculation answer, if you wish to use this in a following calculation.

Examples:

1) Calculate: $\dfrac{1}{4} + \dfrac{2}{5}$

 *Using a calculator*

Give your answer as a decimal

0.65

2) Use your calculator to work out $\sqrt{30 + 80 \times \frac{1}{3}}$

Give your answer as a decimal – write your full calculator display.

10.5039675

3) Use your calculator to work out $(0.85)^3 - 1\frac{1}{5}$

Give your answer as a decimal,
write your full calculator display.

−0.585875

Using a calculator (2)

Practice questions:

Use your calculator to evaluate the following, leaving your full calculator display (8 digits or more):

a) 4.5^2

b) $4 \div 7$

c) $\dfrac{4.5 \times 8}{9^3}$

d) $(1.5 + 1.8)^2 \times 1.07$

e) $\dfrac{4.5 + 8.1}{2.2 \times 1.8}$

f) $\dfrac{\sqrt{3.2}}{2.1 \times 4.98}$

g) $\sin(25)$

h) $\cos(40)$

i) $\tan(20)$

j) $\tan^{-1}(10)$

k) $\cos^{-1}(0.6)$

l) $\sin^{-1}(0.2)$

m) $\sqrt{\dfrac{7}{8}}$

n) $4 - \sqrt[3]{6}$

o) $\dfrac{6\pi}{7}$

p) $\dfrac{3}{7} \times \sqrt{8.4}$

q) $\sqrt{5.6} - 1.2^5$

r) $\dfrac{\sqrt{19.2 + 3.2^2}}{2.6 \times 1.3}$

s) $\dfrac{5^{1.2}}{2} + \dfrac{\sqrt{8.4}}{6}$

t) $\dfrac{4.2^3 + 5.3}{6.4^{0.7}}$

u) $\dfrac{\sqrt[3]{8.4} - 7.5}{1\frac{4}{5}}$

v) $8\frac{1}{9} - \sqrt[4]{80}$

w) $\sqrt[3]{\dfrac{7\pi^2 + 6.8}{2.2^5}}$

x) $\left(\dfrac{\sqrt[5]{9.2} + 8.5}{6.8^{0.4}}\right)^{\pi}$

Exam question:

Use your calculator to work out $\sqrt{30 + 80 \times \frac{1}{3}}$

a) Write down your full calculator display.

b) Round your answer to 3 significant figures.

(1)

Adding and subtracting fractions

To add or subtract fractions you need to have common denominators. You then only need to add/subtract the numerators once the denominators have been made the same.

Example

Calculate: $\dfrac{1}{4} + \dfrac{2}{5}$ We need both denominators to be the same.

The lowest common multiple of 4 and 5 is 20, so we need to change both fractions to an equivalent, so that they both have a denominator of 20. $\dfrac{1}{4} = \dfrac{5}{20}$ $\dfrac{2}{5} = \dfrac{8}{20}$

Once the denominators are the same, we just add the numerators. $\rightarrow$ $\dfrac{5}{20} + \dfrac{8}{20} = \dfrac{5+8}{20} = \dfrac{13}{20}$

Practice questions:

Add the following fractions, leaving your answer in its simplest form:

a) $\dfrac{2}{7} + \dfrac{3}{7}$

b) $\dfrac{1}{4} + \dfrac{1}{2}$

c) $\dfrac{2}{3} + \dfrac{1}{5}$

d) $\dfrac{1}{3} + \dfrac{1}{2}$

e) $\dfrac{1}{4} + \dfrac{3}{7}$

f) $\dfrac{4}{7} + \dfrac{2}{3}$

g) $\dfrac{5}{6} + \dfrac{7}{8}$

h) $\dfrac{2}{5} + \dfrac{6}{7}$

Example

Calculate: $\dfrac{5}{6} - \dfrac{3}{4}$ We use the same process as adding, we need both denominators to be the same.

The lowest common multiple of 4 and 6 is 12, so we need to change both fractions to an equivalent, so that they both have a denominator of 12. $\dfrac{5}{6} = \dfrac{10}{12}$ $\dfrac{3}{4} = \dfrac{9}{12}$

Once the denominators are the same, we just subtract the numerators. $\rightarrow$ $\dfrac{10}{12} - \dfrac{9}{12} = \dfrac{10-9}{12} = \dfrac{1}{12}$

Practice questions:

Subtract the following fractions, leaving your answer in its simplest form:

i) $\dfrac{5}{7} - \dfrac{3}{7}$

j) $\dfrac{3}{4} - \dfrac{1}{8}$

k) $\dfrac{1}{2} - \dfrac{2}{5}$

l) $\dfrac{5}{6} - \dfrac{1}{4}$

m) $\dfrac{5}{7} - \dfrac{3}{5}$

n) $\dfrac{2}{3} - \dfrac{2}{7}$

o) $\dfrac{1}{5} - \dfrac{1}{2}$

p) $\dfrac{4}{7} - \dfrac{3}{4}$

Exam question

Rachel ate one third of a pizza on Saturday and two fifths of the pizza on Sunday.
What fraction of the pizza is left?

(2)

Adding and subtracting mixed numbers

To add or subtract mixed numbers, you can convert the mixed numbers into improper (top-heavy) fractions, and then you find equivalent fractions with common denominators to complete the calculation.

Example

Calculate: $1\frac{2}{3} + 2\frac{1}{2}$ We first convert these to improper fractions. $\rightarrow \quad \frac{5}{3} + \frac{5}{2}$

The lowest common multiple of 3 and 2 is 6, so we need to change both fractions to an equivalent, so that they both have a denominator of 6. $\frac{5}{3} = \frac{10}{6} \qquad \frac{5}{2} = \frac{15}{6}$

Once the denominators are the same, we just add the numerators $\rightarrow \quad \frac{10}{6} + \frac{15}{6} = \frac{10+15}{6} = \frac{25}{6} = 4\frac{1}{6}$

Practice questions:

Add the following mixed numbers, leaving your answer in its simplest form:

a) $1\frac{3}{5} + 2\frac{1}{5}$

e) $1\frac{1}{7} + 2\frac{2}{5}$

b) $4\frac{1}{3} + 2\frac{2}{3}$

f) $4\frac{1}{6} + \frac{5}{7}$

c) $3\frac{1}{2} + 1\frac{5}{6}$

g) $\frac{4}{5} + 2\frac{3}{8}$

d) $1\frac{1}{2} + 2\frac{1}{3}$

h) $4\frac{3}{8} + 5\frac{7}{9}$

Subtract the following mixed numbers, leaving your answer in its simplest form:

i) $3\frac{5}{6} - \frac{4}{6}$

m) $4\frac{1}{5} - 1\frac{4}{7}$

j) $5\frac{1}{3} - 1\frac{1}{3}$

n) $2\frac{4}{11} - 1\frac{5}{6}$

k) $2\frac{2}{7} - \frac{1}{2}$

o) $6\frac{2}{3} - 7\frac{5}{8}$

l) $2\frac{1}{4} - 2\frac{1}{7}$

p) $1\frac{1}{4} - 6\frac{5}{9}$

Exam question

Terry is preparing for a half marathon.

Terry runs $8\frac{1}{3}$ miles on Saturday and $7\frac{2}{5}$ miles on Sunday.

How many miles has he run in total over the weekend?

(2)

Multiplying and dividing fractions

To multiply fractions you need to multiply the numerators and the denominators together. You then need to check to see if the resultant fraction simplifies.

Example
Calculate: $\frac{3}{4} \times \frac{2}{5}$ $\qquad$ $\frac{3}{4} \times \frac{2}{5} = \frac{3 \times 2}{4 \times 5} = \frac{6}{20} = \frac{3}{10}$

Tip: If you are multiplying a whole number you can write it as a fraction by putting it over 1 $\qquad \rightarrow \frac{3}{4} \times 2 = \frac{3}{4} \times \frac{2}{1}$

Practice questions:
Multiply the following fractions. Leave your answer in its simplest form.

a) $\frac{2}{7} \times \frac{3}{7}$

b) $\frac{1}{4} \times \frac{1}{2}$

c) $\frac{2}{3} \times \frac{1}{5}$

d) $\frac{1}{4} \times \frac{3}{7}$

e) $\frac{4}{7} \times \frac{2}{3}$

f) $\frac{5}{6} \times \frac{6}{8}$

g) $\frac{5}{6} \times \frac{8}{10}$

h) $\frac{4}{7} \times \frac{7}{12}$

i) $\frac{5}{24} \times 4$

To divide fractions you need to multiply by the reciprocal (flip) of the second fraction.

Example
Calculate: $\frac{1}{6} \div \frac{3}{4}$ $\quad$ **Flip the second fraction and change the divide to a multiply.** $\rightarrow \frac{1}{6} \times \frac{4}{3}$ $\quad = \frac{1 \times 4}{6 \times 3} = \frac{4}{18} = \frac{2}{9}$

Practice questions:
Divide the following fractions. Leave your answer in its simplest form.

j) $\frac{5}{7} \div \frac{3}{7}$

k) $\frac{3}{4} \div \frac{1}{8}$

l) $\frac{1}{2} \div \frac{2}{5}$

m) $\frac{5}{6} \div \frac{1}{4}$

n) $\frac{5}{7} \div \frac{3}{5}$

o) $\frac{8}{3} \div 6$

p) $\frac{12}{5} \div \frac{24}{15}$

q) $\frac{4}{21} \div \frac{16}{35}$

Example (Mixed numbers)
Calculate: $1\frac{1}{4} \times 1\frac{2}{5}$ $\quad$ **Convert to improper fractions** $\rightarrow \frac{5}{4} \times \frac{7}{5}$ $\quad = \frac{5 \times 7}{4 \times 5} = \frac{35}{20} = \frac{7}{5} = 1\frac{2}{5}$

Practice questions:
Calculate, leave your answer in its simplest form.

r) $1\frac{1}{2} \times 2\frac{1}{3}$

s) $1\frac{3}{5} \times 1\frac{1}{2}$

t) $2\frac{3}{4} \div 3\frac{1}{2}$

u) $2\frac{4}{5} \div 2\frac{2}{3}$

 Exam question

One lap of a racing circuit is $3\frac{3}{4}$ km.

Work out the total distance for $4\frac{1}{2}$ laps.

(2)

Percentages of a quantity (decimal multipliers)

You can use a decimal multiplier to calculate a percentage of a quantity. To do this, you need to convert the percentages into a decimal (divide by 100), and then multiply it by the quantity.

Example   Find 40% of 64   **Step 1:** Convert 40% as a decimal: $40 \div 100 = 0.4$
                                      Step 2: Multiply the original amount by the multiplier: 64×0.4 = **£25.60**

Practice questions:

Calculate:

a) 40% of £32

b) 50% of £128

c) 50% of £72

d) 30% of £32

e) 70% of £742

f) 65% of £23

g) 13% of £42

h) 94% of £864

i) 91% of £562

j) 3% of £34

To increase a number by a percentage, you use the original quantity as 100%, if you increase a quantity by 20% percent, the new percentage will be 120%. We can now use the new percentage as a decimal multiplier.

Example   Increase £80 by 15%   **Step 1:** Work out the new percentage: $(100 + 15) = 115\%$
                                     Step 2: Convert to a decimal: $(115 \div 100) = 1.15$ (decimal multiplier)
                                     Step 3: Multiply this by the original amount: 80×1.15 = **£92**

Practice questions:

Increase the amounts shown by the given percentages using the decimal multiplier.

k) £24 by 50%

l) £120 by 10%

m) £52 by 50%

n) £60 by 25%

o) £92 by 45%

p) £90 by 7%

q) £32 by 26%

r) £99 by 13%

s) £60 by 32%

t) £56 by 94%

To decrease a number by a percentage, you use the original quantity as 100%, if you decrease a quantity by 12% percent, the new percentage will be 78%. We can now use the new percentage as a decimal multiplier.

Example   Decrease 140g by 22%   **Step 1:** Work out the new percentage: $(100 - 22) = 78\%$
                                     Step 2: Convert to a decimal: $(78 \div 100) = 0.78$ (decimal multiplier)
                                     Step 3: Multiply this by the original amount: $140 \times 0.78 = $ **109.2g**

Practice questions:

Decrease the amounts shown by the given percentages using the decimal multiplier.

u) £16 by 50%

v) £42 by 40%

w) £80 by 10%

x) £120 by 25%

y) £68 by 26%

z) £30 by 8%

α) £80 by 72%

β) £74 by 29%

γ) £33 by 53%

δ) £42 by 43%

Finding a percentage increase and decrease

When an amount increases, it could be that we only know the amount it has increased by, and we want to find the *percentage* that it has been increased by.

$$\text{Percentage increase} = \frac{\text{Amount increased}}{\text{Original amount}} \times 100$$

Examples

a) The price of petrol increased from 112p to 119p. Find the percentage increase.

Step 1: Amount increased = 119 − 112 = 7
Step 2: Original amount = 112
Step 3: 7 ÷ 112 x 100 = **6.25%**

b) The price of a painting increased from £250 to £280. Find the percentage increase.

Step 1: Amount increased = 280 − 250 = 30
Step 2: Original amount = 250
Step 3: 30 ÷ 250 x 100 = **12%**

Practice questions:
Find the percentage increase when an amount has increased from:

a) £60 to £66

b) £120 to £132

c) £50 to £100

d) £50 to £65

e) £140 to £182

f) £52 to £85.28

g) £62 to £65.72

h) £97 to £142.59

i) £87 to £96.57

j) £53 to £64.62

When an amount decreases, we treat it exactly the same way as we did when it increased. we find the amount it decreased by and apply a similar formula.

$$\text{Percentage decrease} = \frac{\text{Amount decreased}}{\text{Original amount}} \times 100$$

Examples

a) The weight of a chocolate bar went down from 72g to 63g. Find the percentage decrease.

Step 1: Amount decreased = 72 − 63 = 9
Step 2: Original amount = 72
Step 3: 9 ÷ 72 x 100 = **12.5%**

b) The value of a car decreased from £25k to £18k. Find the percentage decrease.

Step 1: Amount decreased = 25 − 18 = 7
Step 2: Original amount = 25
Step 3: 7 ÷ 25 x 100 = **28%**

Practice questions:
Find the percentage decrease when an amount has decreased from:

k) £50 to £25

l) £80 to £60

m) £50 to £35

n) £80 to £4

o) £130 to £39

p) £64 to £46.08

q) £28 to £15.40

r) £68 to £59.84

s) £92 to £34.96

t) £78 to £76.32

Exam question:
Clarissa buys a dress and gets £39.60 discount off the full price.
The dress was originally priced at £180 pounds.
What was her percentage discount?

(2)

Compound interest

Compound interest means that each time interest is paid, the added interest also receives interest from then on. Put simply, as an amount grows each period (usually each year), so does the interest.

Example

Jim invests £200 with a fixed compound interest rate of 5% each year

a) How much money will he have after 4 years?

After year 1 : Jim has £200 x 1.05 = £210

After year 2 : Jim has £210 x 1.05 = £220.50   = 200 x 1.05 x 1.05   = 200 x 1.05^2

After year 3 : Jim has £220.50 x 1.05 = £231.525   = 200 x 1.05 x 1.05 x 1.05   = 200 x 1.05^3

After year 4 : Jim has £231.525 x 1.05 = **£243.10**   = 200 x 1.05 x 1.05 x 1.05 x 1.05   = 200 x 1.05^4

b) How much money will he have after 20 years?

You can continue the pattern for up to 20 years, but using the multiplier allows you to do it quickly

200 x 1.05^{20} = **£530.66**

Compound Interest Formula	x = interest rate as a decimal (e.g. 5% = 0.05)
Amount after "n" years = $a(1 \pm x)^n$	a = initial amount n = number of years

Example 2

I invest £500 at a 10% interest rate, how many years will it be until I have over £1000?

$a = 500$, $x = 0.10$, $n = ?$ **Trial** different values of n until we go over £1000.

After 7 years: 500 x $(1 + 0.10)^7$ = 974.36

After 8 years: 500 x $(1 + 0.10)^8$ = 1071.79   →   It will take 8 years until I have **over** £1000.

Practice questions:

State how much money you will you have, if you invest:

Give your answers to the nearest penny

a) £200 at a compound interest rate of 10%, after 3 years.

b) £200 at a compound interest rate of 20% after 2 years.

c) £350 at a compound interest rate of 12% after 3 years.

d) £64 at a compound interest rate of 15% after 5 years.

e) £112 at a compound interest rate of 8% after 7 years.

f) £632 at a compound interest rate of 0.5% after 8 years.

g) I invest £300 at a 10% interest rate, how many years will it be until I have over £3000?

h) I invest £900 at a 7% interest rate, how many years will it be until I have over £2000?

Exam question:

Mischa invests £40,000 in a long-term investment plan.

The account pays 1.3% compound interest per year.

Work out the value of his investment after 5 years.

Give your answer to the nearest penny.

(2)

Appreciation and depreciation

Appreciation means an object gains in value each year and is treated the same as compound interest.

Example

Chip bought a property for £240,000. His local estate agent informs him that his property will have appreciated 5% for every year he has owned it. Chip has owned it for 8 years.

How much is Chip's property now worth according to his estate agent, to the nearest pound?

Using the compound interest formula → 240,000 x $(1.05)^8$ = **£354,589**

Practice questions:

How much, to the nearest penny, will a property be worth if:

a) It was originally worth £250,000 and it appreciates at a rate of 9% per year, for 4 years.

b) It was originally worth £320,000 and it appreciates at a rate of 4% per year, for 5 years.

c) It was originally worth £420,000 and it appreciates at a rate of 3% per year, for 5 years.

d) It was originally worth £750,000 and it appreciates at a rate of 0.5% per year, for 8 years.

Depreciation means an object loses in value each year and is also treated the same as compound interest.

Example

A £20,000 car depreciates by 15% each year. How much will the car be worth after 5 years?

Since the car value goes down the decimal multiplier in the bracket of the formula is 1 – 0.15 = 0.85

Using the compound interest formula → 20,000 x $(0.85)^5$ = **£8,874.11**

Practice questions:

How much, to the nearest penny, will a car be worth if:

e) It was originally worth £40,000 and it depreciates at a rate of 10% per year, for 5 years.

f) It was originally worth £25,000 and it depreciates at a rate of 8% per year, for 4 years.

g) It was originally worth £18,000 and it appreciates at a rate of 4% per year, for 3 years.

h) It was originally worth £22,000 and it appreciates at a rate of 2.5% per year, for 6 years.

Exam question:

The value of a campervan depreciates by 12% each year.
If the campervan is currently valued at £18,000.
How many full years will it take to be **less than half** of its current price?

(2)

Reverse percentages

When reversing a percentage, your need to know the current percentage as the original percentage was 100%. We divide the amount by the current percentage to find 1%, and then multiply that by 100 to get to the original 100% amount.

Example (price increased)
The price of a Bluetooth speaker has increased by 20% to £72.
What was the original price?

Step 1: Current percentage = 100% + 20% = 120%
Step 2: 1% = 72 ÷ 120 = 0.60
Step 3: 100% = 0.60 x 100 = **£60**

Alternate: Using decimal multiplier (120% = 1.20) → £72 ÷ 1.20 = **£60**

You can check your solution by calculating 20% of your answer and adding it on.

Practice questions:
What is the original amount if a price was:

a) Increased by 10%, and is now £66

b) Increased by 25%, and is now £40

c) Increased by 20%, and is now £60

d) Increased by 15%, and is now £46

e) Increased by 5%, and is now £126

f) Increased by 12%, and is now £71.68

g) Increased by 62%, and is now £37.26

Example (price decreased)
A calculator was reduced in price by 30% to £8.40.
What was the original price?

Step 1: Current percentage = 100% - 30% = 70%
Step 2: 1% = 8.40 ÷ 70 = 0.12
Step 3: 100% = 0.12 x 100 = **£12**

Alternate: Using decimal multiplier (70% = 0.70) → £8.40 ÷ 0.70 = **£12**

NOTE:
You cannot work out 30% and add it on.

Practice questions:
What is the original amount if a price was:

h) Decreased by 10%, and is now £63

i) Decreased by 25%, and is now £36

j) Decreased by 5%, and is now £76

k) Decreased by 20%, and is now £104

l) Decreased by 35%, and is now £156

m) Decreased by 3%, and is now £143.56

n) Decreased by 52%, and is now £21.84

Exam question:
Jess answered 80% of the questions in a test correctly.
She answered 60 of the questions correctly.
Work out the total number of questions in the test.

(2)

Laws of indices

If two numbers are given with powers and you **multiply** them, as long as the bases (big numbers) of are the same, you can just add the powers.

$$7^a \times 7^b = 7^{a+b}$$

Examples

a) $4^3 \times 4^4 = 4 \times 4 \times 4 \quad \times \quad 4 \times 4 \times 4 \times 4 = 4^7$

b) $7^5 \times 7^3 = 7^{5+3} = 7^8$

c) $2 \times 2^3 = 2^1 \times 2^3 = 2^{1+3} = 2^4$

d) $5^4 \times 5^3 \times 5^3 = 5^{4+3+3} = 5^{10}$

NOTE : $x^0 = 1$ Anything to the power 0 is always 1.

$x^1 = x$ Anything to the power 1, is the same as itself and a power 1 is often not written.

Practice questions:

Simplify:

a) $2^2 \times 2^4$

b) $3^5 \times 3^2$

c) $6^2 \times 6^8$

d) $x^3 \times x^4$

e) $8^6 \times 8$

f) $2^7 \times 2^{-2}$

g) $9^7 \times 9^{-4}$

h) $2^{-8} \times 2^4$

i) $5^{-4} \times 5^2$

j) $x^{-8} \times x^5$

k) $4^2 \times 4^{-2}$

l) $7^{-5} \times 7^{-4}$

m) $x^{-2} \times x^{-5}$

n) $2^0 \times 2^5$

o) $y^{-2} \times y^{-2}$

If two numbers are given with powers and you **divide** them, as long as the bases (big numbers) are the same, you can just subtract the powers.

$$7^a \div 7^b = 7^{a-b}$$

Examples

a) $4^7 \div 4^4 = 4^{7-4} = 4^3$

b) $7^5 \div 7^3 = 7^{5-3} = 7^2$

c) $2^3 \div 2 = 2^3 \div 2^1 = 2^{3-1} = 2^2$

d) $5^4 \times 5^3 \div 5^3 = 5^{4+3-3} = 5^4$

HINT: You must be very careful using index laws and the rules of subtracting that you follow the rules of adding and subtracting with negative numbers. The rules still apply e.g. $7^5 \div 7^{-3} = 7^{5--3} = 7^{5+3} = 7^8$

Practice questions:

Simplify:

p) $2^4 \div 2^2$

q) $3^5 \div 3^2$

r) $6^8 \div 6^2$

s) $x^4 \div x^3$

t) $8^6 \div 8$

u) $2^{-7} \div 2^2$

v) $9^{-7} \div 9^4$

w) $2^{-8} \div 2^4$

x) $5^4 \div 5^{-2}$

y) $x^8 \div x^{-5}$

z) $4^2 \div 4^{-2}$

α) $7^{-5} \div 7^{-4}$

β) $x^{-2} \div x^{-5}$

γ) $2^0 \div 2^{-5}$

δ) $y^2 \div y^{-2}$

HINT: Remember that a fraction line between a numerator and a denominator means divide.

Exam question:

Simplify the following leaving as powers of **a**, **b** and **c**

$$\frac{a^5 b^6 c^4}{a^2 b^2 c}$$

(3)

Laws of indices (part 2)

When you need to find the power of another power, you multiply the powers together.

$$(7^a)^b = 7^{a \times b}$$

Examples

a) $(4^3)^2 = 4 \times 4 \times 4 \ \times 4 \times 4 \times 4 = 4^6$

b) $(7^3)^3 = (7 \times 7 \times 7) \times (7 \times 7 \times 7) \times (7 \times 7 \times 7) = 7^{3 \times 3} = 7^9$

c) $(2^4)^3 = 2^{4 \times 3} = 2^{12}$

d) $(3^{-4})^5 = 3^{-4 \times 5} = 3^{-20}$

Practice questions:

Simplify:

a) $(2^5)^2$

b) $(5^7)^3$

c) $(3^6)^3$

d) $(8^2)^3$

e) $(2^5)^{-2}$

f) $(4^{-4})^3$

g) $(6^2)^{-3}$

h) $(9^2)^{-3}$

i) $(3^0)^8$

j) $(4^4)^{-4}$

k) $(7^{-2})^{-2}$

l) $(5^0)^{-2}$

Any number / value to the power zero is equal to 1

$$x^0 = 1$$

When fractions are used with a power, the power is applied to both numerator and denominator

$$\left(\frac{x}{y}\right)^a = \frac{x^a}{y^a}$$

Examples

a) $\left(\frac{2}{3}\right)^2 = \frac{2^2}{3^2} = \frac{4}{9}$

b) $\left(\frac{3}{4}\right)^3 = \frac{3^3}{4^3} = \frac{27}{64}$

c) $\left(1\frac{1}{5}\right)^2 = \left(\frac{6}{5}\right)^2 = \frac{6^2}{5^2} = \frac{36}{25} = 1\frac{11}{25}$

Practice questions:

Simplify:

m) $\left(\frac{2}{5}\right)^2$

n) $\left(\frac{3}{4}\right)^2$

o) $\left(\frac{5}{6}\right)^2$

p) $\left(\frac{4}{7}\right)^2$

q) $\left(\frac{1}{3}\right)^3$

r) $\left(\frac{2}{8}\right)^2$

s) $\left(1\frac{1}{3}\right)^2$

t) $\left(1\frac{1}{2}\right)^2$

u) $\left(1\frac{3}{4}\right)^2$

v) $\left(2\frac{1}{4}\right)^2$

w) $\left(3\frac{1}{2}\right)^2$

x) $\left(3\frac{1}{3}\right)^3$

Exam question:

Calculate the following, leaving your answer as simple as possible.

$$\left(\frac{2}{3}\right)^2 \times \left(\frac{1}{2}\right)^3$$

(3)

Laws of indices (harder)

If you are multiplying two expressions together you need to multiply the numbers as normal and use index laws with the letters (add the powers).

Example

Simplify: $6a^6b \times 8a^3b^4$ $6 \times 8 = 48$ $a^6 \times a^3 = a^9$ $b \times b^4 = b^5$ **Answer: $48a^9b^5$**

Practice questions:

Simplify:

a) $4a^5b^4 \times 7a^2b^8$

b) $9x^5y^8 \times 5x^6y$

c) $8pq^8 \times 3p^5q^9$

d) $2x^8y^3 \times 12x^6y^7$

e) $7a^8b \times 7a^8b$

f) $4p^7q^5 \times 13pq$

g) $6x^{-2}y^7 \times 4x^5y$

h) $7a^9b^4 \times 8a^8$

i) $3x^{-5}y^4 \times 14x^{-1}y$

If you are dividing two expressions you need to divide the numbers as normal and use index laws with the letters (subtract the powers).

Example

Simplify: $\dfrac{24x^7y^2}{3x^3y^6}$ $24 \div 3 = 8$ $x^7 \div x^3 = x^4$ $y^2 \times y^6 = y^{-4}$ **Answer: $8x^4y^{-4}$**

Practice questions:

Simplify:

j) $\dfrac{20x^8y^{12}}{5x^4y^9}$

k) $\dfrac{48x^9y^8}{6x^2y}$

l) $\dfrac{32a^5b^7}{8a^4b^3}$

m) $\dfrac{30x^6y^9}{3x^6y^5}$

n) $\dfrac{64x^6y^8}{16xy^5}$

o) $\dfrac{90b^4c^9}{15b^7c^3}$

p) $\dfrac{28x^{10}y^2}{4x^{10}y^8}$

q) $\dfrac{54v^9w^7}{9v^{12}w^8}$

r) $\dfrac{56x^{-4}y^6}{7x^7y^{-3}}$

If you are raising an expression to a power you need to raise the number to the power as normal and use index laws with the letters (multiply the powers).

Example

Simplify: $(4a^6b)^3$ $4^3 = 64$ $(a^6)^3 = a^{18}$ $(b)^3 = b^3$ **Answer: $64a^{18}b^3$**

Practice questions:

Simplify:

s) $(6x^4y^7)^2$

t) $(5a^8b)^2$

u) $(2x^9y^2)^3$

v) $(9g^3h^8)^2$

w) $(3mn^5)^3$

x) $(2x^6y^{11})^4$

y) $(5x^{-4}y^{12})^3$

z) $(8ab^4c^{-9})^2$

α) $(2x^{12}y^7z)^5$

Exam question:

Simplify: $\dfrac{12x^5y^6 \times 4xy^7}{8x^8y^2}$

(3)

Negative indices

A **negative** power means you take the reciprocal. You then calculate the power as a normal positive power.

Examples

a) Calculate 5^{-2}

Means $\dfrac{1}{5^2} = \dfrac{1}{25}$

b) Calculate 4^{-3}

Means $\dfrac{1}{4^3} = \dfrac{1}{64}$

c) Calculate 3^{-1}

Means $\dfrac{1}{3^1} = \dfrac{1}{3}$

d) Calculate 3^{-3}

Means $\dfrac{1}{3^3} = \dfrac{1}{27}$

Practice questions:

Evaluate the following:

a) 8^{-2}

b) 2^{-5}

c) 7^{-1}

d) 5^{-3}

e) 6^{-2}

f) 9^{-2}

g) 9^{-1}

h) 6^{-3}

i) 4^{-1}

j) 2^{-4}

k) 1^{-3}

l) 3^{-4}

Examples

a) Simplify a^{-2}

Means $\dfrac{1}{a^2}$

b) Simplify $(4x)^{-3}$

Means $\dfrac{1}{(4x)^3} = \dfrac{1}{64x^3}$

c) Simplify $4x^{-3}$

Practice questions:

Simplify the following:

m) y^{-2}

n) d^{-4}

o) x^{-1}

p) p^{-3}

q) k^{-7}

r) h^{-2}

s) z^{-8}

t) y^{-1}

u) c^{-5}

v) $(3y)^{-2}$

w) $(7x)^{-2}$

x) $3t^{-3}$

y) $(4y)^{-3}$

z) $5x^{-2}$

α) $(5x)^{-2}$

β) $9x^{-5}$

γ) $(6y)^{-3}$

δ) $8x^{-2}$

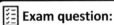 Exam question:

Simplify:

i) $x^7 \times x^5$

ii) a^{-3}

(2)

Product of prime factors

The rule of prime factorisation states that any integer greater than 1 can be written as product of its prime factors. For example 12 – can be written as 2 x 2 x 3 (all prime numbers).
The method for finding the product of prime factors is often done by using "prime factor trees".

Example

Express 60 as a product of its prime factors.

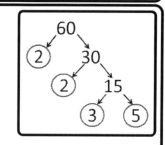

Step 1: Divide 60 by a factor that is not 1 – in this case (2) → 60 ÷ 2 = 30
Step 2: Circle any prime numbers prime number (2)
Step 3: Now divide the remaining number (30) which is not prime – again, by a factor that is not 1 (2) → 30 ÷ 2 = 15
Step 4: Repeat until all the numbers are circled (and are prime)
Step 5: Now write the product of all those numbers that are circled: 2 x 2 x 3 x 5
Step 6: Where there is a repetition of a prime number, index form must be used: **2^2 x 3 x 5**

Practice questions:

Express the following numbers as a product their prime factors:

a) 24

b) 30

c) 40

d) 27

e) 70

f) 108

g) 56

h) 132

Exam question:

Write 800 as a product of its prime factors
using index notation.

(3)

15

HCF and LCM using Venn diagrams

Venn diagrams and the product of prime factors can be used to determine the highest common factor (HCF) and lowest common multiple (LCM) of 2 or more numbers.

Example

Find the HCF and LCM of 24 and 36.

Step 1: Write as products of prime factors

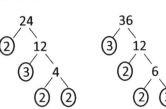

$24 = 2 \times 2 \times 2 \times 3$ $36 = 2 \times 2 \times 3 \times 3$

Step 2: Put the prime factors that are in both into the middle of a Venn diagram.

Step 3: Put the left over numbers into the sides of the Venn diagram.

For HCF: Multiply the numbers in the middle section of the diagram: $2 \times 2 \times 3 = 12$

For LCM: Multiply all the numbers in the diagram: $2 \times 2 \times 2 \times 3 \times 3 = 72$

HCF = 12

LCM = 72

Practice questions:

a) Find the HCF and LCM of 24 and 30.

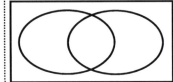

HCF = ...

LCM = ...

b) Find the HCF and LCM of 15 and 33.

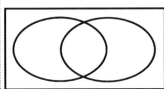

HCF = ...

LCM = ...

c) Find the HCF and LCM of 20 and 44.

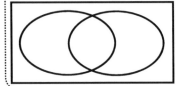

HCF = ...

LCM = ...

d) Find the HCF and LCM of 32 and 40.

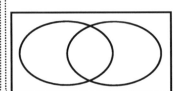

HCF = ...

LCM = ...

e) Find the HCF and LCM of 54 and 72.

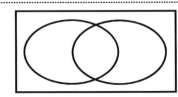

HCF = ...   LCM = ...

Practice questions:

f) Find the HCF and LCM of 88 and 96.

HCF = ...

LCM = ...

g) Find the HCF and LCM of 112 and 76.

HCF = ...

LCM = ...

h) Find the HCF and LCM of 146 and 104.

HCF = ...

LCM = ...

i) Find the HCF and LCM of 120 and 184.

HCF = ...

LCM = ...

j) Find the HCF and LCM of 10, 16 and 18.

HCF = ...

LCM = ...

k) Find the HCF and LCM of 14, 21 and 35.

HCF = ...

LCM = ...

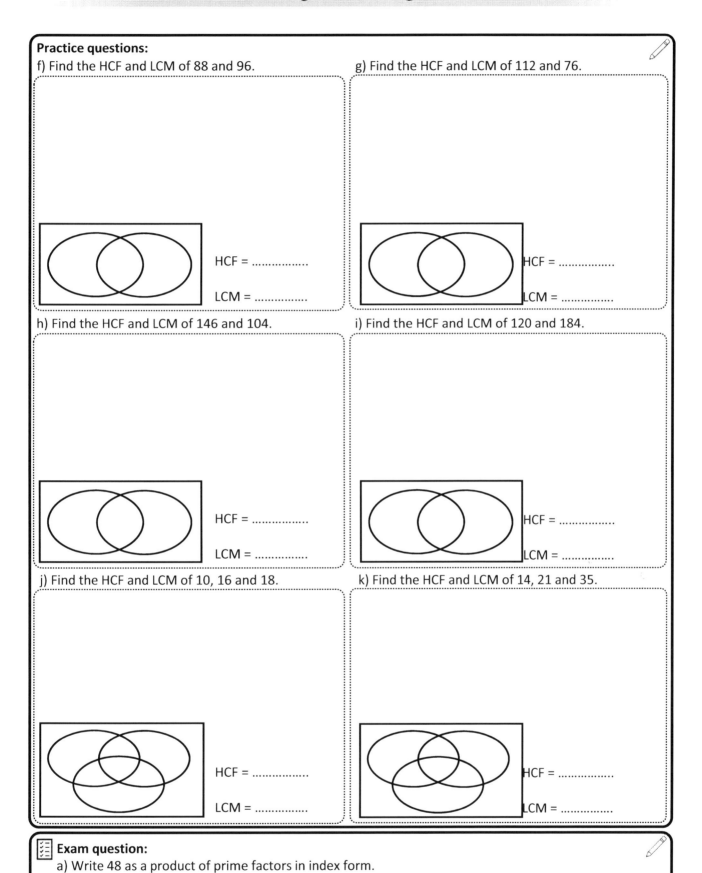

Exam question:

a) Write 48 as a product of prime factors in index form.

b) Find the lowest common multiple of 48 and 22.

(3)

HCF and LCM from index form

Venn diagrams and the product of prime factors can be used to determine the highest common factor (HCF) and lowest common multiple (LCM) of 2 or more numbers.

Example

Find the HCF and LCM of A and B

$A = 2^3 \times 3^2 \times 7$ $B = 2 \times 3^4 \times 5$

Step 1: Write in long form to make it easier to see the numbers.

  $A = 2 \times 2 \times 2 \times 3 \times 3 \times 7$ $B = 2 \times 3 \times 3 \times 3 \times 3 \times 5$

Step 2: Put the prime factors that are in both into the middle of a Venn diagram.

Step 3: Put the left over numbers into the sides of the Venn diagram

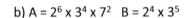

For HCF: Multiply the numbers in the middle section of the diagram: $2 \times 3 \times 3 = 18$

HCF = 18

For LCM: Multiply all the numbers in the diagram: $2 \times 2 \times 7 \times 2 \times 3 \times 3 \times 3 \times 3 \times 7 = 31752$ **LCM = 31752**

Practice questions:

Find the HCF and LCM of A and B.

a) $A = 2^4 \times 3 \times 5^3$ $B = 2^2 \times 3^4 \times 5^2$

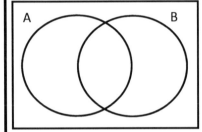

HCF:

LCM:

b) $A = 2^6 \times 3^4 \times 7^2$ $B = 2^4 \times 3^5$

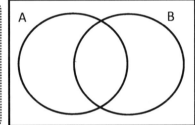

HCF:

LCM:

c) $A = 3^2 \times 5^2 \times 7^4$ $B = 3^2 \times 5 \times 7^3 \times 11$

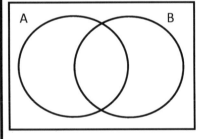

HCF:

LCM:

d) $A = 2^5 \times 5^3 \times 7^4$ $B = 2 \times 3^2 \times 7^3$

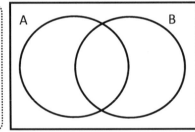

HCF:

LCM:

e) $A = 2^5 \times 3^3 \times 13^2$ $B = 2^3 \times 3 \times 13^2$

HCF:

LCM:

f) $A = 2 \times 3^5 \times 5^4 \times 7^3$ $B = 3^2 \times 5 \times 7^4 \times 11$

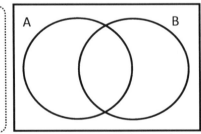

HCF:

LCM:

Exam question:

$A = 3^5 \times 5^3 \times 11^2$ $B = 3 \times 5^4 \times 11^4$

a) Find the highest common factor of A and B.

b) Find the lowest common multiple of A and B.

(3)

HCF and LCM from index form (harder)

Sometimes you may need to write numbers as powers of their prime factors before using a Venn diagram.

Example

Find the HCF and LCM of A and B

$A = 8 \times 3^5$ $B = 32 \times 3^2$

Step 1: Write 8 and 32 as powers of 2. $2^3 = 8$ $2^5 = 32$

 $A = 2^3 \times 3^5$ $B = 2^5 \times 3^2$

Step 2: Put the prime factors that are in both into the middle of a
         Venn diagram.

Step 3: Put the left over numbers into the sides of the Venn diagram

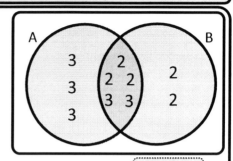

For HCF: Multiply the numbers in the middle section of the diagram: $2 \times 2 \times 2 \times 3 \times 3 = 72$

HCF = 72

For LCM: Multiply all the numbers in the diagram: $3 \times 3 \times 3 \times 2 \times 2 \times 2 \times 3 \times 3 \times 2 \times 2 = 7776$

LCM = 7776

Practice questions:

Find the HCF and LCM of A and B.

a) $A = 16 \times 5^4$ $B = 2 \times 5^6$

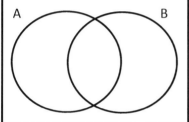

HCF:

LCM:

b) $A = 3 \times 7^3$ $B = 81 \times 7^6$

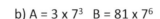
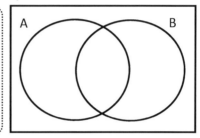

HCF:

LCM:

c) $A = 4 \times 3^2 \times 5$ $B = 64 \times 3^5 \times 5^3$

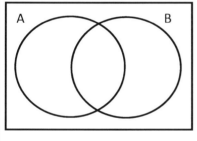

HCF:

LCM:

d) $A = 125 \times 3^2 \times 7^3$ $B = 3^4 \times 5 \times 7^2$

HCF:

LCM:

e) $A = 2 \times 81 \times 121$ $B = 128 \times 3 \times 11$

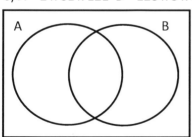

HCF:

LCM:

f) $A = 32 \times 25 \times 49$ $B = 2 \times 625 \times 343$

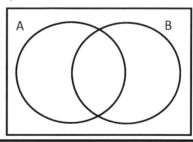

HCF:

LCM:

Exam question:

$A = 27 \times 5^{51}$ $B = 9 \times 5^{23}$

a) Find the highest common factor of A and B.

b) Express the number $A \div B$ as a product of its prime factors.
   Give your answer in its simplest form.

(3)

19

Unitary ratios

Ratios are easier to compare in the form 1:n. To put a ratio in the form 1:n, you must divide the ratio by the first number. This is often used as an easy way to compare values and for scaling.

Example

Write the following in the form 1:n

a) 5:8   Divide both values by 5 → **1 : 1.6**   b) 8 : 3   Divide both values by 8 → **1 : 0.375**

Practice questions:

Write in the form 1 : n

a) 2 : 10

b) 3 : 21

c) 8 : 36

d) 10 : 5

e) 5 : 2

f) 12 : 18

g) 5 : 24

h) 2 : 6 : 9

i) 18 : 16

Example

A recipe for 10 buns uses 120g of flour. How much flour do you need to make 24 buns?

Step 1: The ratio of buns to flour is 10 : 120   **Divide by 10**

Step 2: Unitary ratio: 1 : 12   **So you need 12g of flour for 1 bun**

Step 3: Scale up   24 : 288   **Multiply by 24 for 24 buns**

So you need 288g of flour to make 24 buns.

Practice questions:

Use the recipe sheet provided to answer the following questions.

How much of Butter do you need to make:

j) 20 scones?

l) 1 scone?

k) 5 scones?

m) 3 scones?

How much of Milk do you need to make:

n) 5 scones?

p) 7 scone?

o) 1 scone?

q) 28 scones?

Scones Recipe
(Makes 10 Scones)

Ingredients

200g Plain Flour
50g Butter
20g Caster Sugar
140ml Milk

How many scones could you make with an unlimited supply of other ingredients, but only:

r) 50g of caster sugar?

t) 500ml of milk?

s) 40g of butter?

u) 450g of plain flour?

Exam question:

Timothy has a recipe for making Cornflake cakes.
The recipe uses 120g of chocolate and 80g of Cornflakes to make 12 cakes.

a) How much chocolate should Timothy use to make 30 cakes?

b) Timothy has plenty of Cornflakes, but only 500g of chocolate, what is the maximum number of Cornflake cakes he can make?

(3)

Unitary ratio – best value/comparisons

Unitary ratios can be used to compare different scenarios including offers and multibuy deals.

Example

Which is better value: 5 pens for £1.40 or 12 pens for £3.40

Step 1 : Write as ratios.   5 : 1.40   12 : 3.40
Step 2 : Write as unitary ratios.   1 : 0.28   1 : 0.2833

So **5 pens for £1.40 is better value** as 1 pen cost 28p, compared to the 12 pens where 1 pen cost 28.3p.

Practice questions:

Which is better value? (you must show your working).

a) 2 pens for 40p or
   5 pens for 90p

b) 4 chocolate bars for £6 or
   6 chocolate bars for £8

c) 5 bottles of wine for £29 or
   7 bottles of wine for £41

d) 24 sweets for £3.26 or
   32 sweets for £4.34

Example

It takes 3 people 4 hours to seal 1200 envelopes
How long will it take 2 people to seal 600 envelopes?
Step 1 : Summarise the scenario 3 people take 4 hours for 1200 envelopes
Step 2 : Change the information to reflect the question : 1 person takes 12 hours for 1200 envelopes
                                                              2 people take 6 hours for 1200 envelopes
So it would take 3 hours.   2 people take 3 hours for 600 envelopes

Practice questions:

It takes 5 builders 12 hours to build a 2m high wall.

e)   If 3 builders worked at the same rate, how long
     would it take them to build a 2m high wall?

f)   If 8 builders worked at the same rate, how long
     would it take them to build a 4m high wall?

g)   If 6 builders worked at the same rate, how long
     would it take them to build a 3m high wall?

Exam question:

Two local shops sell cupcakes at different prices.
Candy's Cakes sells 8 cupcakes for £6.
Patty's Patisserie sells 5 cupcakes for £4.50.
Which is better value?
You must show all your working.

8 cupcakes
£6.00

5 cupcakes
£4.50

(3)

Ratio

Ratios are simplified in a similar way to fractions. To simplify a ratio you need to find the highest common factor of both numbers in the ratio and divide them both by that factor.

Example

Simplify 12:30

Step 1: Find the highest common factor of 12 and 30   HCF of 12 and 30 = 6

Step 2: Divide both sides by this number   12 : 30 → **2 : 5**

$\div 6 \left(\begin{array}{c} 12 : 30 \\ 2 : 5 \end{array} \right) \div 6$

Practice questions:

Fully simplify the following ratios.

a) 4 : 6

b) 10 : 6

c) 3 : 9

d) 20 : 14

e) 9 : 15

f) 20 : 28

g) 14 : 42

h) 48 : 54

i) 60 : 52

j) 112 : 88

k) 10 : 6 : 12

l) 9 : 15 : 21

To share an amount using ratios you need to add the numbers in the ratio to see how many parts there are, then divide the amount to be split by this number to find the value of 1 part. You then multiply by the value of 1 part by each of the numbers given in the ratio.

Example

Share £60 in the ratio 3:7

Step 1: 3 + 7 = 10, so there are 10 parts altogether

Step 2: £60 ÷ 10 = £6, so <u>1 part is worth £6</u>

Step 3: The first person gets £6 x 3 = **£18**   The second person gets £6 x 7 = **£42**

> You can check your answers by adding them up. They should add up to the original amount.

Practice questions:

Share the following amounts into the given ratios.

m) £20 in the ratio 1 : 4

n) £20 in the ratio 3 : 7

o) £32 in the ratio 3 : 5

p) £32 in the ratio 3 : 1

q) £48 in the ratio 5 : 1

r) £48 in the ratio 7 : 5

s) £200 in the ratio 3 : 7

t) £72 in the ratio 5 : 3

u) £132 in the ratio 1 : 2 : 3

v) £205 in the ratio 1 : 2 : 2

Exam question:

Write the area of shape A : area of shape B as a ratio.
Give your answer in its simplest form.

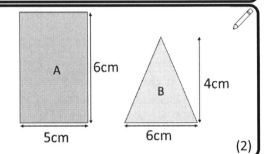

A   6cm

B   4cm

5cm   6cm

(2)

Sometimes you need to find the amount shared and you are given information to allow you to attain this.

Example

Some money was shared in the ratio 3:5
The first person received £21
a) How much was shared out?

b) How much did the second person get?

a) The first person got 3 parts which was £21
1 part is £21 ÷ 3 = £7
Total parts = 3 + 5 = 8 parts
Therefore 8 parts = £7 x 8 = **£56**

b) The second person gets 5 parts = £7 x 5 = **£35**

Practice questions:

Find the value of the money that was shared out.

a) Some money was shared in the ratio 4:5.
   The first person received £16.

b) Some money was shared in the ratio 2:3.
   The first person received £12.

c) Some money was shared in the ratio 7:4.
   The first person received £28.

d) Some money was shared in the ratio 1:2:3.
   The second person received £32.

Example

At a rugby game the ratio of men : women is 12 : 5
There are 4200 **more** men than women.
Work out the number of people at the game.

The 4200 is represented by the difference in the ratios so 12 − 5 = 7 parts which is 4200
1 part is 4200 ÷ 7 = 600 people
Total parts = 12 + 5 = 17 parts
Therefore 17 parts = 17 x 600 = **11,200**

Practice questions:

Find the number of people at these football matches if:

e) The ratio of men : women is 3 : 2.
   There were 8,000 more men than women.

f) The ratio of men : women is 5 : 8.
   There were 3,000 more women than men.

g) The ratio of men : women is 11 : 2.
   There were 4,500 more men than women.

h) The ratio of men : women is 5 : 7
   There were 1,500 more men than women.

i) The ratio of men : women is 9 : 2
   There were 2,100 more men than women.

Exam question:

Alex, Ben and Clare take a test.
The ratio of Alex's score to Ben's score is 7 : 5
Alex scored 10 more marks than Ben.
Alex scored 3 more marks than Clare.
Work out Clare's score.

(2)

Ratio as a fraction

When amounts are shared in a ratio, you need to be able to work out the fraction of the total that each person receives.
To do this you need to add up the parts of the ratio to find the total.
The total of the parts will be the denominator of the fraction

Example

Phoebe and Felix share some sweets in the ratio 5:3.

a) What fraction of the sweets does Phoebe get?

Find the total number of parts: 5 + 3 = 8

Phoebe gets 5 parts of the ratio out of 8 so write this as a fraction.

Answer: $\dfrac{5}{8}$

b) What fraction of the sweets does Felix get?

Felix gets 3 parts of the ratio out of 8 so write this as a fraction.

Answer: $\dfrac{3}{8}$

Practice questions:

Boris and Matt share some money in the following ratios. What fraction of the money does Boris get?

a) 7:2

b) 8:5

c) 9:7

d) 1:8

e) 6:5

f) 5:6

g) 11:9

h) 13:15

i) 6:17

j) 14:5

k) 27:19

l) 31:7

Practice questions:

Sally and Emily share some sweets in the following ratios. What fraction of the money does Emily get?

m) 8:7

n) 6:9

o) 2:11

p) 7:9

q) 13:4

r) 9:11

s) 13:6

t) 8:15

u) 1:14

v) 17:19

w) 28:15

x) 23:32

Practice questions:

Ed, Pete and Tim share some money in the following ratios. What fraction of the money does Ed get?

y) 5:4:6

z) 3:5:7

α) 2:9:12

β) 5:7:8

γ) 2:9:5

δ) 7:9:4

ε) 11:17:12

μ) 10:15:19

π) 15:2:18

Exam question:

There are only rectangular and circular biscuits in a tin.
The ratio of rectangles to circles is 8:11.
What fraction of the biscuits are circles?

(1)

Combining ratios

In order to combine ratios with a common part, you need the common part to have the same value.

Example

The ratio of pigs to sheep is 3 : 4
The ratio of sheep to cows is 7 : 5
Find the ratio of pigs : cows

| Check your answer to see if it simplifies! |

Both ratios have sheep in them so we need to make that part the same in both ratios.
The LCM of 4 and 7 is 28.

x7 ⤸ 3 : 4 ⤸ x7   x4 ⤸ 7 : 5 ⤸ x4
      21 : 28   28 : 20

You can now combine the ratios
The ratio of pigs : cows = **21 : 20**

Practice questions:

Find the ratio **a : c** if:

a) The ratio of a : b is 4 : 1
   and the ratio of b : c is 2 : 3

b) The ratio of a : b is 3 : 5
   and the ratio of b : c is 1 : 4

c) The ratio of a : b is 6 : 1
   and the ratio of b : c is 6 : 7

d) The ratio of a : b is 4 : 3
   and the ratio of b : c is 5 : 2

e) The ratio of a : b is 6 : 2
   and the ratio of b : c is 9 : 5

Example

The ratio of pigs to sheep is 7:2
The ratio of sheep to cows is 3:1
There are 3480 animals in total.
How many are pigs?

Pigs : Sheep : Cows

×3 ⤸ 7 : 2
        3 : 1 ⤸ ×2
    21 : 6 : 2

21 + 6 + 2 = 29 parts
3480 ÷ 29 = 120
120 x 21 = pigs = **2520**

Practice questions:

In each case, there are 3000 buttons in the colours blue, red and green.

f) The ratio of red : blue is 5 : 1
   and the ratio of blue : green is 2 : 3
   How many blue buttons are there?

g) The ratio of red : blue is 5 : 3
   and the ratio of blue : green is 2 : 8
   How many green buttons are there?

h) The ratio of red : blue is 4 : 3
   and the ratio of blue : green is 1 : 6
   How many red buttons are there?

Exam question:

The ratio of dogs to cats is 8:5
The ratio of cats to rabbits is 3:7
There are 72 dogs.
How many animals are there in total?

(3)

Rounding numbers to significant figures

When rounding to significant figures, you must first determine which is the 1st significant figure.
The first significant figure is the first digit which is not a zero when read from left to right.
All other digits after the 1st significant figures are significant and should be counted, even if they are a zero.
The method of rounding is no different once you have identified which digit you are rounding to.

HINT: When rounding to significant figures, there answer may require zero place holders to retain size.

Example – rounding to significant figures

a) 4.62 to 2 significant figures.   **Answer = 4.6**

The number 4 is the 1st significant figure, so 6 is the 2nd significant figure. Since the following digit (2) is **less than 5**, you leave the 6 and remove the 2 after it.

b) 207.1 to 2 significant figures.   **Answer = 210**

The number 2 is the 1st significant figure, so 0 is the 2nd significant figure. Since the following digit (7) is **5 or more**, you raise the 0 to a 1 and remove the digits after. Include a zero place holder.

c) 0.00654 to 1 significant figure.   **Answer = 0.007**

The number 6 is the 1st significant figure. Since the following digit (5) is **5 or greater**, you raise the 6 to a 7 and remove the digits after.

Practice questions:

Round the following values to **1 significant figure**:

a) 4.58   b) 7.519   c) 42.58   d) 0.0327

e) 25.78   f) 0.781   g) 725.12   h) 0.0582

i) 6543   j) 2.043   k) 24535   l) 468.23

m) 79.65   n) 4256   o) 0.0047   p) 199.67

Round the following values to **2 significant figures**:

a) 2.578   b) 0.781   c) 785.12   d) 1082

e) 5831   f) 9.709   g) 79.87   h) 0.40282

i) 5030   j) 6843   k) 0.5083   l) 0.03374

m) 46.42   n) 6.861   o) 2.994   p) 3986.3

Round the following values to 3 **significant figures**:

a) 43422.6   b) 700.85   c) 6754.36

d) 0.004539   e) 0.55052   f) 0.07008

g) 60842   h) 0.48961   i) 39.9703

Exam question:

Pi is given as 3.14159265358979323846.....

Round pi to   a) 2 significant figures.

b) 7 significant figures.

(2)

When estimating calculations, the iGCSE expectation is that you round **each** term you are working with to 1 significant figure. Then only work with those values. Any other estimation will not get you the marks.

Example – estimating calculations by rounding to significant figures

a) Estimate 4.8×3.1 When rounded to 1 significant figure = $4.8 \rightarrow 5$ and $3.1 \rightarrow 3$
The estimation is therefore $5 \times 3 = 15$ **Answer = 15**

b) Estimate: $\dfrac{448}{14.2}$ When rounded to 1 significant figure = $448 \rightarrow 400$ and $4.2 \rightarrow 10$
The estimation is therefore $\dfrac{400}{10} = 40$ **Answer = 40**

c) Estimate: $\dfrac{16.2 \times 346}{0.474}$ Rounding to 1 significant figure gives: $\dfrac{20 \times 300}{0.5} = \dfrac{6000}{0.5} = 12000$ **Answer = 12000**

Practice questions:

Estimate the solutions to these calculations:

a) 54.6×2.54

b) 165×12.5

c) $\dfrac{16.74}{3.65}$

d) 3525×563.2

e) $\dfrac{4367}{176.3}$

f) $6.7^2 \times 22$

g) $\dfrac{58.74 - 8.67}{1.956}$

h) $\dfrac{\sqrt{8.72}}{2.43}$

i) $\dfrac{8.46 \times 19.4}{3.94}$

j) $\dfrac{642}{13.2 \times 1.87}$

k) $\dfrac{9.7^2}{2.1^2}$

l) $\dfrac{32 \times 386}{1.56 \times 62.1}$

m) $\dfrac{58.54 \times 621}{27.3}$

n) $\dfrac{19.7^3}{7.83}$

o) $\dfrac{43.6 \times 76.2}{0.098}$

p) $\dfrac{0.065 \times 0.195}{2.254}$

q) $\dfrac{0.082 \times 46.8}{368 \times 0.472}$

r) $\dfrac{36.2 + 4.42}{0.487}$

Exam question:

Charlene buys 78 packets of crisps at 31p each.
Estimate the total cost in pounds.

(2)

Upper and Lower bounds

When a number is rounded, the upper bound is the limit of the largest value which would round to that number. The lower bound is the smallest value which would round to the number.

Example: A TV is 32 inches, to the *nearest inch*, find the upper and lower bounds of the TV size.

The **lower bound** will be the smallest value which would round **up** to 32, which would be 31.5 inches
The **upper bound** will be the limit of the largest value which would round **down** to 32, which would be 32.5 inches as the actual largest number would be 32.499999....

Lower bound = 31.5 inches   Upper bound = 32.5 inches

 The range of numbers which could be rounded can be written as an inequality.
So if we state that the TV size is called x then the range of potential value is written: $31.5 \leq x < 32.5$

When working with bounds, special attention needs to be paid to the level of accuracy in the question. e.g. nearest 10, whole numbers/integers, decimal places, significant figures, etc.

Practice questions:

Find the upper and lower bounds of the following lengths which have been rounded to the nearest cm.

a) 6 cm

b) 18 cm

c) 20 cm

d) 88 cm

e) 3 cm

f) 11 cm

g) 54 cm

h) 100 cm

Find the upper and lower bounds of the following weights which have been rounded to 1 decimal place.

i) 3.4 kg

j) 7.2 kg

k) 11.5 lb

l) 13.6 g

m) 18.8 oz

n) 6.0 mg

Find the upper and lower bounds of the following distances which have been rounded to 1 significant figure.

o) 7 m

p) 9 cm

q) 30 ft

r) 80 mm

s) 500 m

t) 100 cm

u) 0.9 km

v) 7000 m

Exam question

Geoff has estimated the dimensions of his room as shown to the nearest metre.

What is the minimum perimeter that the room could be if measure accurately?

5m

3m

(2)

Standard Form

Standard form is used to represent very large or very small numbers. You must have one number before the decimal point which is multiplied by a power of 10 (a number between 1 and 10).

Example (larger numbers)
Write 2400 in standard form.
Step 1: We want to write it as 2.4×10^n
Step 2: Identify how many tens you need to **multiply** 2.4 by to get 2400 $\qquad 2.4 \times 10 \times 10 \times 10 = 2400$
Step 3: Now write in standard form where the n is the number of 10s needed $\rightarrow \mathbf{2.4 \times 10^3}$

Practice questions:
Convert these numbers into standard form:

a) 300

b) 700

c) 2000

d) 720

e) 9000

f) 5400

g) 34000

h) 65,000

i) 532,000

j) 505,000

k) 7,050,300

l) 58,001,000

Example (small numbers)
Write 0.0567 in standard form.
Step 1: We want to write it as 5.67×10^{-n} (n is negative as it is going to be divided by 10s, but it will still be written as $\times 10^{-n}$
Step 2: Identify how many tens you need to **divide** 5.67 by to get 0.00567 $\qquad 5.67 \div 10 \div 10 = 0.0567$
Step 3: Now write in standard form where the n is the number of 10s needed $\rightarrow \mathbf{5.67 \times 10^{-2}}$

Practice questions:
Convert these numbers into standard form:

m) 0.05

n) 0.008

o) 0.56

p) 0.0086

q) 0.00523

r) 0.0208

s) 0.000009

t) 0.000501

u) 0.000042

v) 0.0000008

w) 0.000115

x) 0.00010005

Exam question:
a)   Write 546,000,000 in standard form.

b)   Write 0.000000381 in standard form.

(2)

Calculating with standard form

When calculating with standard form, it my be easier to convert back to ordinary numbers to work with. When multiplying or dividing you can re-arrange the powers of 10 in the calculation to make it easier.

Example (adding /subtracting with standard form)
Calculate $2.3 \times 10^5 + 5 \times 10^4$
Step 1: Convert to ordinary numbers → 230,000 + 50000
Step 2: Now you can just add together using column method or otherwise → 280,000
Step 3: Now write in standard form → $\mathbf{2.8 \times 10^5}$

Practice questions:
Calculate, leaving your answer in standard form:

a) $2 \times 10^5 + 4 \times 10^4$

b) $6 \times 10^6 + 2 \times 10^5$

c) $4.7 \times 10^6 + 2.2 \times 10^7$

d) $2.9 \times 10^5 + 3.2 \times 10^4$

e) $7.6 \times 10^4 - 2.8 \times 10^3$

f) $4.8 \times 10^8 - 3.7 \times 10^7$

Example (multiplying/dividing with standard form)
Calculate $(5 \times 10^5) \times (3.2 \times 10^3)$
Step 1: Re-arrange to put both numbers first and powers of 10 second. $5 \times 3.2 \times 10^5 \times 10^3$
Step 2: Multiply the numbers and then the powers of 10. 16×10^8
Step 3: Put back into standard form. $1.6 \times 10 \times 10^8$ $= \mathbf{1.6 \times 10^9}$

Practice questions:
Calculate, leaving your answer in standard form:

g) $(2 \times 10^5) \times (4 \times 10^4)$

h) $(6 \times 10^5) \div (2 \times 10^3)$

i) $(2 \times 10^4) \times (1.4 \times 10^3)$

j) $(3.2 \times 10^7) \div (8 \times 10^4)$

k) $(7.2 \times 10^9) \times (1.2 \times 10^4)$

l) $(1.6 \times 10^5) \times (8.1 \times 10^8)$

Exam question:

Work out $\dfrac{8.2 \times 10^7}{2 \times 10^4}$

Leave your answer in standard form.

(2)

30

Exchange rates

An exchange rate allows you to change money to different currencies.
To convert to another currency you must **multiply** by the exchange rate.
To convert back from another currency you must **divide** by the exchange rate.

£1 = $1.4 →

£1 = $1.4 ←

Examples

Using the exchange rate of £1 = $1.4
a) What is £25 in dollars?   £25 x 1.4 = **$35**   b) What is $84 in pounds? $84 ÷ 1.4 = **£60**

Practice questions:

Convert the following currencies using the rates shown.

£1 = $1.3	£1 = ¥143	£1 = €1.12

£1 = 93.84 Rupees	£1 = 18.7 Rand

a) £50 to dollars ($)

b) £200 to Euros (€)

c) £40 to Yen (¥)

i) 700 Rupees to pounds

d) £600 to Rand

j) 870 Rand to pounds

Hint: Convert to pounds first

e) £480 to Rupees

k) $400 to Euros (€)

f) $520 to pounds

g) €50 to pounds

l) €300 to Yen (¥)

h) ¥5000 to pounds

When dealing with problems with exchange rates, its best to first convert everything to the same currency.

Example

A phone costs £263 in the UK and ₱6448 in Mexico. Where is it cheaper?

£1 = ₱24.8

Step 1: Change ₱6448 to pounds so you can compare the prices → ₱6448 ÷ 24.8 = £260
Step 2: Now compare the two values: £260 < £263, so it is **cheaper in Mexico** (by £3).

Practice questions:

You must show all your working.

£1 = $1.3	£1 = ₱24.8	£1 = €1.12

m) A shirt cost £32 in the UK and $42.90 in the USA. Where was it cheaper?

n) A camera cost £84 in the UK and €89.60 in France. Where was it cheaper?

o) An game cost £8.49 in the UK and ₱200 in Mexico. Where is it cheaper?

p) A watch cost £144.89 in the UK and $190 in the USA. Where is it cheaper?

Exam question:

Theresa bought a pair of sunglasses in the USA. She paid $32.50.
In the UK, an identical pair of sunglasses costs £24.99.
In which country were the sunglasses cheaper, and by how much?
Show all your working.

£1 = $1.32

(2)

Substitute numbers into algebraic expressions/formulae

When substituting, you need to 'replace' letters with the given numbers.
Please note: If a number is next to a letter, e.g. **4a**, it means **4** multiplied by **a**.
It is exactly the same process when substituting numbers into expressions or formula, but when substituting numbers into a formula, you are likely to be trying to find out the value of the remaining variable.
You are also more likely to have more than one variable to substitute into a formula.

Examples

Evaluate these expressions when n = 2

a) $n + 6 = 2 + 6 = 8$ **Answer : 8**

b) $5 - n = 5 - 2 = 3$ **Answer : 3**

c) $5 + 3n = 5 + 3(2) = 5 + 6 = 11$ **Answer : 11**

d) $n^3 = (2)^3 = 2 \times 2 \times 2 = 8$ **Answer : 8**

A formula for s is given as $s = \frac{d}{t}$
Find the value of when s, when :

e) d = 20 and t = 10 : $s = \frac{20}{10} = 2$ **Answer : 2**

f) d = 16 and t = 2 : $s = \frac{16}{2} = 8$ **Answer : 8**

g) d = 14 and t = 4 : $s = \frac{14}{4} = 3.5$ **Answer : 3.5**

Practice questions:
Evaluate these expressions when $n = 6$

a) $5n$

b) $n + 5$

c) $10 - n$

d) $\frac{n}{2}$

e) $n - 2$

f) $8n - 4$

g) $20 - 3n$

h) n^2

i) $n^2 + 5n$

Practice questions:
Given that $r = 3$, $s = 9$, $t = 4$ and $w = 10$, find the value of v:

j) $v = \frac{t+16}{5}$

k) $v = 4s + 2$

l) $v = \frac{t}{2} + 2$

m) $v = 4r + w$

n) $v = tw + r$

o) $v = r^2 + s$

Please note: When substituting with negative numbers, you need to be extremely careful that you do not miss where there are two negatives, as this is a common error amongst learners. $2 - (-3) = 5$

Practice questions:
Evaluate these expressions when $n = -2$

p) $4n$

q) $n - 4$

r) $2n + 2$

s) $10 - n$

t) $20 - 3n$

u) n^2

Practice questions:
Given that $a = -2$, $b = 12$, $c = -8$ and $d = -7$, find the value of e:

v) $e = a + c$

w) $e = 2d + a$

x) $v = \frac{c-2}{5}$

y) $e = a + c - d$

z) $e = cd$

Δ) $e = abc$

Exam question:
The formula shown converts temperature from Fahrenheit to Celsius.
Work out temperature in Celsius if:
a) the temperature is 86° F
b) the temperature is 14 ° F

Converting Celsius to Fahrenheit

$$T(°C) = \frac{T(°F) - 32}{1.8}$$

(2)

Writing formulas

A formula links several variables together. A formula will always have an equals sign.

Example

Cakes cost £5 each and coffees cost £3 each.
Tim buys x cakes and y coffees.
The total cost is £T.
Write a formula for T in terms of x and y.

Total cost of x cakes: 5 x x = $5x$
Total cost of y coffees: 3 x y = $3y$

You must include 'T =' to get full marks

Answer: $T = 5x + 3y$

Practice questions:

a) Pens cost £6 each.
   Pencils cost £2 each.
   Lois buys p pens and q pencils.
   The total cost is £C.
   Write a formula for C in terms of p and q.

b) Pizzas cost £8 each.
   Chips cost £2 per portion.
   Clark buys p pizzas and c portions of chips.
   The total cost is £A.
   Write a formula for A in terms of p and c.

c) Burgers cost £5 per pack.
   Sausages cost £3 per pack.
   Cara buys b burgers and s sausages.
   The total cost is £K.
   Write a formula for K in terms of b and s.

d) Necklaces cost £60 each.
   Watches cost £150 each.
   Jason buys n necklacess and w watches.
   The total cost is £J.
   Write a formula for J in terms of n and w.

e) Sandwiches cost £4.50 each.
   Crisps cost £1.50 each.
   Bruce buys s sandwiches and c crisps.
   The total cost is £T.
   Write a formula for T in terms of s and c.

f) Pears cost 80p each.
   Oranges cost £1.10 each.
   Diana buys r pears and s oranges.
   The total cost is £F.
   Write a formula for F in terms of r and s.

g) Pens cost £3 each. Pencils cost £1.50 each.
   Rubbers cost £2.50 each.
   Barry buys a pens, b pencils and c rubbers.
   The total cost is £P.
   Write a formula for P in terms of a, b and c.

h) Apples cost 80p each. Bananas cost £1.20 each.
   Coconuts cost £3.70 each.
   Victor buys x apples, y bananas and z coconuts.
   The total cost is £C.
   Write a formula for C in terms of x, y and z.

i) Arthur buys pens for £3 each.
   He sells them for £7 each.
   He buys x pens and sells y pens.
   His total profit is £P.
   Write a formula for P in terms of x and y.

j) Lex buys chocolates for £4.50 each.
   He sells them for £9.60 each.
   He buys c chocolates and sells d chocolates.
   His total profit is £X.
   Write a formula for X in terms of c and d.

Expanding and Simplifying brackets

To expand and simplify you must first expand both brackets separately then simplify your answer by collecting like terms.

Example

Expand and simplify: $2(4x + 1) + 4(x + 5)$

$$= 8x + 2 + 4x + 20$$
$$= 9x + 22$$

Expand the first bracket: $2(4x + 1) = 8x + 2$

Expand the second bracket : $+4(x + 5) = +4x + 20$

Answer : $9x + 22$

Practice questions:

Expand and simplify the following expressions:

a) $4(x + 3) + 3(x + 5)$

b) $5(x + 6) + 2(x - 4)$

c) $3(x - 4) + 6(x - 2)$

d) $6(2x + 5) + 3(x + 8)$

e) $7(x + 2) + 8(5x - 3)$

Example

Expand and simplify: $2(7x + 1) - 6(x - 4)$

$$= 14x + 2 - 6x + 24$$
$$= 8x + 26$$

Expand the first bracket: $2(7x + 1) = 14x + 2$

Expand the second bracket: $-6(x - 4) = -6x + 24$

$(-6 \times -4 = +24)$

Answer : $8x + 26$

Be careful with the negatives!

Practice questions:

Expand and simplify the following expressions:

f) $2(x + 7) - 3(x + 5)$

g) $4(x + 3) - 6(x - 4)$

h) $8(x - 1) - 3(x + 6)$

i) $7(x + 6) - 5(3x - 4)$

j) $5(2x - 3) - 9(x - 4)$

k) $6(5x - 6) - 7(x + 2)$

l) $9(x + 5) - 3(2x - 7)$

m) $8(3x - 5) - 4(3x + 1)$

n) $6(x + 5) - (x - 3)$

o) $3(4x - 4) - 5(4x - 1)$

Exam question:

Expand and simplify: $8(x - 4) - 6(x + 3)$

(2)

Factorising linear expressions

Factorising means we are putting an expression into brackets. When factorising an expression you need to find the largest whole number and/or letter which goes into all the terms (highest common factor).

Example

Fully factorise the expression : $4x + 8$

$4x + 8$ — Find the largest whole number which is a factor of 4 and 8.   (4)

$4(\quad)$ — The 4 goes on the outside of the brackets.

You then need to divide each term by 4. → $4x \div 4 = x$, $+8 \div 4 = +2$

$4(x + 2)$ — Ensure that you check the sign between the terms being divided.

Answer : $4(x + 2)$

Note: If you do not factorise the expression using the highest common factor, it will not be classed as "fully" factorised, so ensure you have found the highest common factor to achieve full marks.

Practice questions:

Fully factorise the following expressions:

a) $5x + 5$

b) $6k - 30$

c) $15h + 25$

d) $14a - 49$

e) $20 + 10y$

f) $24x + 20$

g) $27a + 9b$

h) $20x - 45y$

i) $72x + 27$

j) $60y - 144$

k) $12k - 36m$

l) $18a + 24p$

m) $64x - 72y$

n) $14a + 7b - 21c$

o) $5x + 10y - 15z$

Examples

Factorise: $3x^3 - 9x^2$ — Find the largest whole number which is a factor of 3 and 9.   (3)

Find the highest power of x which goes into both terms. (x^2)

$3x^2(\quad)$ — The 3 and x^2 go on the outside of the brackets.

You then need to divide each term by $3x^2$. → $3x^3 \div 3x^2 = x$, $-9x^2 \div 3x^2 = -3$

$3x^2(x - 3)$ — Ensure that you check the sign between the terms being divided.

Answer : $3x^2(x - 3)$

Practice questions:

Fully factorise the following expressions:

p) $3x^2 + 3x$

q) $6k^2 - 24k$

r) $20x + 5xy$

s) $32a^2 + 8ab$

t) $24x^3 - 36x^2$

u) $24x^2 + 20xy$

v) $27a^3 + 18a^2$

w) $28x^2 + 44x$

x) $5x^2 - 20x + 10xy$

y) $20a^2b + 10a - 50abc$

Exam question: Fully factorise $12x^2 - 32x$

(2)

35

Factorising linear expressions (2)

Factorising means we are putting an expression into brackets. When factorising an expression you need to find the largest whole number and/or letter which goes into **all** the terms (highest common factor).

Examples

Factorise: $20x^3y - 8x^2y^4$

$4x^2y(\quad)$

$4x^2y(5x - 2y^3)$

Step 1: Find the largest whole number which is a factor of 20 and 8. (4)
Step 2: Find the highest power of x and y which goes into <u>both</u> terms. (x^2y)
Step 3: $4x^2y$ goes on the outside of the brackets.
Step 4: Divide each term by $4x^2y$ to find what goes in the bracket.

Answer : $4x^2y(5x - 2y^3)$

Note: If you do not factorise the expression using the highest common factor, it will not be classed as "fully" factorised, so ensure you have found the highest common factor to achieve full marks.

Practice questions:

Fully factorise the following expressions:

a) $18a^5b^2 + 24a^5b^3c^4$

b) $6p^5q^4r^2 - 27p^3q^3$

c) $30a^2b^3c^5 + 120a^4b$

d) $36m^3n^4 - 54m^5np^2$

e) $20r^3s^4 + 40rs^5$

f) $12a^4bc - 54a^3b^2c^3$

g) $6n^5pq - 20n^5p^4q^3$

h) $16stv^4 + 32s^3t^2$

i) $25k^3m^4 - 20k^3m$

j) $9c^4d^3 + 12c^4d$

k) $2v^5w^4x^2 + 8v^5wx^4$

l) $15w^4x^3y^5 + 49wx^4$

m) $24s^2t^4 + 36s^5t^5$

n) $35x^2y + 28x^5y^3$

o) $4r^4st^3 - 10rs^2t^5$

p) $6hk^3 + 18h^2k^2$

q) $50p^3q^4r^4 - 80p^5q^5$

r) $12b^5c + 3b^2c^4d$

s) $35d^4e^3f^5 + 63d^2e^5f^5$

t) $7v^4w^4 - 84v^3w^2x^4$

Exam question:

Fully factorise $36xy^6z^4 - 24x^4y^7z^4$

(2)

Solving equations that include a bracket

To solve an equation with brackets, you can expand the brackets first, and then rearrange or you could divide by the value outside of the bracket (if possible).

Examples: Solve the following equations.

a) $3(x + 2) = 18$ Divide both sides by 3.
    $x + 2 = 6$ Subtract 2 from both sides.
       x = 4

Alternatively

    $3(x + 2) = 18$ Expand the bracket.
    $3x + 6 = 18$ Subtract 6 from both sides.
      $3x = 12$ Divide both sides by 3.
       x = 4

b) $2(4x - 5) = 70$ Divide both sides by 2.
    $4x - 5 = 35$ Add 5 to both sides.
      $4x = 40$ Divide both sides by 4.
       x = 10

Alternatively

    $2(4x - 5) = 70$ Expand the bracket.
    $8x - 10 = 70$ Add 10 to both sides.
      $8x = 80$ Divide both sides by 8.
       x = 10

Practice questions:

Solve:

a) $5(x + 2) = 25$

b) $7(x + 3) = 42$

c) $2(x + 4) = 22$

d) $6(x - 3) = 36$

e) $2(x - 9) = 28$

f) $5(x - 7) = 25$

g) $2(3x + 1) = 26$

h) $4(3x + 7) = 64$

i) $2(4x - 1) = 62$

j) $4(4x - 5) = 92$

k) $-3(x + 1) = 18$

l) $3(-4x + 7) = 45$

Exam question:

The rectangle has two dimensions as shown in the diagram (units are in cm).
The area is 26 cm².
Find the value of x.

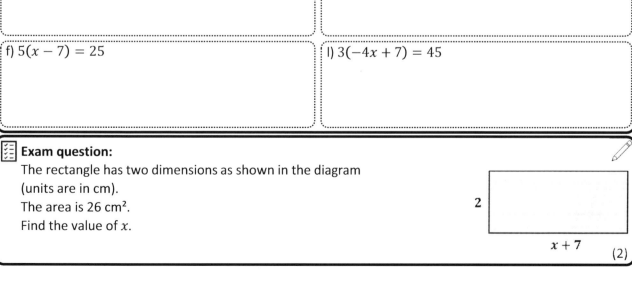

(2)

37

Solving equations that include two brackets

To solve an equation with more than one bracket, you are likely to have to expand and simplify both brackets first, before solving a two step equation.

Examples: Solve the following equations.

Be careful with the last sign!

a) $2(x + 3) + 3(x + 5) = 46$ Expand the brackets
$2x + 6 + 3x + 15 = 46$ Simplify the terms
$5x + 21 = 46$ Subtract 21
$5x = 25$ Divide by 5
$x = 5$

$\boxed{-4x - 1 = +4}$

b) $6(x + 2) - 4(x - 1) = 30$ Expand the bracket
$6x + 12 - 4x \boxed{+ 4} = 30$ Simplify the terms
$2x + 16 = 30$ Subtract 16
$2x = 14$ Divide by 2
$x = 7$

Practice questions:

Solve:

a) $2(x + 3) + 4(x + 1) = 28$

e) $2(3x + 6) + 4(x + 2) = 50$

i) $5(x + 4) - 2(x + 3) = 32$

b) $5(x + 2) + 3(x + 2) = 24$

f) $3(2x - 3) + 2(3x + 1) = 53$

j) $8(x + 3) - 5(x + 1) = 28$

c) $6(x + 1) + 4(x - 3) = 14$

g) $5(x + 3) + 2(3x + 1) = 83$

k) $9(x + 2) - 3(x - 5) = 45$

d) $3(x - 2) + 3(x - 5) = 3$

h) $3(3x + 3) + 2(2x - 1) = 98$

l) $4(3x - 2) - 2(4x + 1) = 2$

Exam question:

The shape shown has some dimensions given (units are in cm).

The area is 115 cm².

Find the value of x.

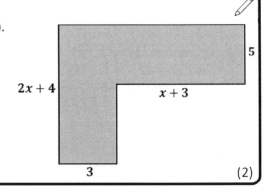

$2x + 4$

$x + 3$

5

3

(2)

Solving equations that include powers

To solve equations with powers you need to do the inverse which is to square root.
There will be two solutions, the positive and negative square roots.

Examples:

a) Solve: $x^2 = 25$

$\qquad x = \pm\sqrt{25} \qquad\qquad x = 5 \text{ or} -5$

b) Solve: $\qquad x^2 + 5 = 14$

$\qquad\qquad\qquad x^2 = 9$

$\qquad\qquad\qquad x = \pm\sqrt{9} \qquad\qquad x = 3 \text{ or} -3$

Practice questions:

Solve:

a) $x^2 = 4$

b) $x^2 = 64$

c) $x^2 = 100$

d) $x^2 = 121$

e) $x^2 = 81$

f) $x^2 = 225$

Practice questions:

Solve:

g) $x^2 + 6 = 31$

h) $x^2 + 8 = 12$

i) $x^2 + 8 = 24$

j) $x^2 - 7 = 74$

k) $x^2 - 5 = 4$

l) $x^2 + 12 = 156$

Practice questions:

Solve:

m) $3x^2 = 12$

n) $2x^2 = 128$

o) $6x^2 = 54$

p) $4x^2 = 144$

q) $4x^2 + 3 = 67$

r) $2x^2 - 12 = 150$

s) $9x^2 + 9 = 90$

t) $3x^2 - 15 = 60$

 Exam question:

The triangle has two dimensions as shown in the diagram (units are in cm).

The area is 294 cm².

Find the value of x.

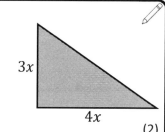

$3x$

$4x$

(2)

Solving equations with the unknown on both sides

To solve an equation with an unknown on both sides of an equation, you first add/subtract the smallest number of unknowns to remove it from one of the sides. You will then have a two step equation.

Examples: Solve the following equations.

a) 3x + 4 = x + 16   Subtract x from both sides

   2x + 4 = 16   Subtract 4 from both sides

   2x = 16   Divide both sides by 2

   x = 8

b) 4x − 1 = 23 − 2x   Add 2x to both sides

   6x − 1 = 23   Add 1 to both sides

   6x = 24   Divide both sides by 6

   x = 4

Practice questions:

Solve:

a) $3x + 2 = 2x + 8$

f) $4x + 1 = 2x + 9$

k) $3x + 9 = 24 - 2x$

b) $2x + 6 = x + 13$

g) $4x - 4 = x + 20$

l) $13x - 8 = x + 64$

c) $4x + 5 = 3x + 34$

h) $8x + 10 = 4x + 2$

m) $15x - 38 = 4x - 5$

d) $4x - 11 = 3x + 13$

i) $10x - 33 = x + 21$

n) $5x + 13 = -4x - 50$

e) $6x + 11 = 7x + 13$

j) $4x - 5 = 8x + 43$

o) $x - 11 = 9x - 75$

Exam question: Not to scale

The length of two identical lines are shown (in cm).

Find the value of x.

⟵ $9x + 13$ ⟶

⟵ $4x + 58$ ⟶

(2)

Solve equations with the unknown on both sides in brackets

You must first expand the brackets before moving the unknowns to one side.

Examples : Solve the following equations

a) $5(x + 7) = 3(x - 5)$ Expand the brackets

   $5x + 35 = 3x - 15$ Subtract 3x from both sides

   $2x + 35 = -15$ Subtract 35

   $2x = -50$ Divide by 2

   x = −25

b) $13x - 6 = 5(2x + 6)$ Expand the brackets

   $13x - 6 = 10x + 30$ Subtract 10x from both sides

   $3x - 6 = 30$ Add 6

   $3x = 36$ Divide by 3

   x = 12

Practice questions:

Solve the following equations:

a) $4(x - 4) = 3x$

b) $7x = 2(x + 5)$

c) $5(x + 4) = x + 44$

d) $7(2x + 3) = 9x + 56$

e) $13x - 14 = 4(2x + 9)$

f) $5(x + 1) = 4(x + 3)$

g) $3(x + 3) = 2(x + 8)$

h) $6(x - 2) = 4(x + 1)$

i) $8(x - 1) = 3(x + 4)$

j) $2(5x + 6) = 7(x + 6)$

k) $7(3x - 2) = 4(4x + 9)$

l) $4(x + 6) = 5(x + 4)$

m) $6(x - 3) = 3(3x + 2)$

n) $4(3x - 5) = 7(2x + 8)$

o) $6(4x - 3) = 3(9x + 6)$

Exam question:

The areas of the two rectangles shown are equal.

Find the value of x.

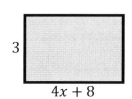

$4x + 8$

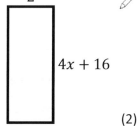

$4x + 16$

(2)

41

Solve equations with unknowns on both sides with fractions

You must first multiply by the denominator before moving the unknowns to one side.

Example:

Solve: $\dfrac{8x+6}{3} = 2x+9$

First multiply both sides by 3.

Then solve to equation with x on both sides as previously.

$8x + 6 = 3(2x + 9)$

$8x + 6 = 6x + 27 \qquad (-6x)$

$2x + 6 = 27 \qquad\qquad (-6)$

$2x = 21 \qquad\qquad\; (\div 2)$

$x = \dfrac{21}{2}$ **or** $10\dfrac{1}{2}$

Don't assume the answers will always be integers

Practice questions:

Solve the following equations:

a) $\dfrac{5x+8}{2} = 2x + 7$

e) $\dfrac{2x-9}{6} = 4x - 1$

i) $4x + 2 = \dfrac{7-2x}{4}$

b) $\dfrac{7x-4}{5} = x + 4$

f) $9x + 2 = \dfrac{8x-12}{5}$

j) $\dfrac{7-x}{5} = 8x - 2$

c) $5x - 7 = \dfrac{2x+5}{3}$

g) $\dfrac{5x-10}{5} = 6x + 3$

k) $2 - 3x = \dfrac{9-4x}{7}$

d) $8x + 3 = \dfrac{11x+5}{4}$

h) $7x - 9 = \dfrac{8x-12}{2}$

l) $\dfrac{4-8x}{6} = 24 - 3x$

Exam question:

The following shape is a square.

Find the value of x.

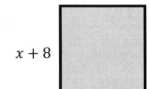

$x + 8$

$\dfrac{5x - 3}{4}$

(3)

Solve equations with unknowns on both sides with fractions (2)

You must first multiply by the denominators before moving the unknowns to one side.

Example:

Solve: $\dfrac{8x+6}{3} = \dfrac{2x+9}{4}$

First multiply both sides by 3 and 4

Then solve to equation with x on both sides as previously.

$4(8x+6) = 3(2x+9)$

$32x + 24 = 6x + 27$

$26x + 24 = 27 \qquad (-6x)$

$26x = 3 \qquad (-24)$

$x = \dfrac{3}{26} \qquad (\div 26)$

Don't assume the answers will always be integers

Practice questions:

Solve the following equations:

a) $\dfrac{5x+2}{2} = \dfrac{2x+28}{4}$

e) $\dfrac{6x-5}{5} = \dfrac{3x+4}{2}$

i) $\dfrac{3x+3}{4} = \dfrac{8-2x}{9}$

b) $\dfrac{2x-6}{4} = \dfrac{2x+5}{6}$

f) $\dfrac{4x-3}{6} = \dfrac{5x-2}{9}$

j) $\dfrac{4+x}{7} = \dfrac{4x-9}{3}$

c) $\dfrac{6x+8}{3} = \dfrac{5x-7}{3}$

g) $\dfrac{8x-3}{6} = \dfrac{x+4}{2}$

k) $\dfrac{3-2x}{6} = \dfrac{9-4x}{2}$

d) $\dfrac{3x+8}{4} = \dfrac{x+2}{2}$

h) $\dfrac{7x-3}{5} = \dfrac{9x+4}{8}$

l) $\dfrac{1-7x}{7} = \dfrac{3-5x}{11}$

Exam question:

The following shape is a square.

Find the value of x.

$\dfrac{x+7}{2}$

$\dfrac{7x-2}{8}$

(3)

Forming and solving equations

You sometimes have to form an equation to solve a problem.

Example:

Kim has some sweets.
Jim has **4** more sweets than Kim.
Tim has twice as many sweets as Jim.
Altogether there are 100 sweets.
How many sweets does Tim have?

Let Kim have x sweets

Kim: x
Jim: $x + 4$
Tim: $2(x + 4) = 2x + 8$

$$x + (x + 4) + (2x + 8) = 100$$
$$4x + 12 = 100$$
$$4x = 88$$
$$x = 22$$

Form an equation, the total of everyone's sweets equals 100

So Kim has 22 sweets.

Tim has: $2(22) + 8$
$$= 52 \text{ sweets}$$

Practice questions:

a) Sue has some sweets.
Dan has 3 more sweets than Sue.
Len has 4 times as many sweets as Dan. Altogether there are 207 sweets.
How many sweets does Sue have?

b) Sue has some sweets.
Dan has 5 fewer sweets than Sue.
Len has twice as many sweets as Sue.
Altogether there are 67 sweets.
How many sweets does Sue have?

c) Sue has some sweets.
Dan has 9 more sweets than Sue.
Len has 3 times as many sweets as Dan. Altogether there are 101 sweets.
How many sweets does Dan have?

d) Sue has some sweets.
Dan has 7 fewer sweets than Sue.
Len has 6 times as many sweets as Sue. Altogether there are 201 sweets.
How many sweets does Len have?

e) Sue has some sweets.
Dan has 8 more sweets than Sue.
Len has 4 times as many sweets as Sue. Altogether there are 194 sweets.
How many sweets does Dan have?

f) Sue has some sweets.
Dan has twice as many sweets as Sue.
Len has 5 fewer sweets than Dan.
Altogether there are 215 sweets.
How many sweets does Len have?

Exam question:

Karen is 5 years older than Paul.
Steve is 3 times as old as Karen.
The total of their ages is 130.
How old is Karen?

(4)

44

Inequalities on a number line

Inequalities can be represented on a number line. The bounds are represented by dots. A filled in dot ● means it can equal the number (≤ or ≥). An empty dot ○ means it can't equal the number (< or >).

Examples :

a) Represent the inequality $x > 2$ on the number line.

b) Represent the inequality $x \leq 3$ on the number line.

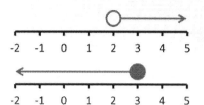

Practice questions:
Represent the following inequalities on the number line.

a) $x < 2$

b) $x \leq 4$

c) $x > 5$

d) $x \leq 0$

e) $x \geq -2$

f) $x > -2$

g) $x \leq -3$

h) $-2 > x$

i) $-4 \leq x$

j) $x \geq 0$

Examples :

c) Represent the inequality $-1 \leq x < 1$ on the number line.

b) Represent the inequalities $x < 0$ or $x \geq 4$ on the number line.

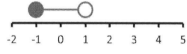

Practice questions:
Represent the following inequalities on the number line.

k) $1 < x < 4$

l) $0 < x \leq 3$

m) $-1 \leq x < 2$

n) $x < -1$ or $x \geq 4$

o) $x \leq 2$ or $x > 4$

p) $x < 0$ or $x > 1$

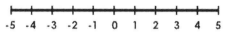

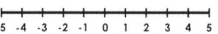
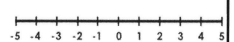
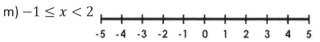
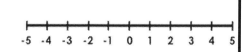

Inequalities on a number line (2)

You are sometimes asked to write the inequality which is represented on a number line. You must make sure your inequalities are pointing the correct direction.

Examples:

Write down the inequality represented on the number line:

a)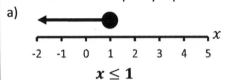

$x \leq 1$

b)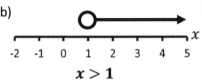

$x > 1$

c)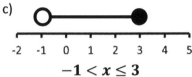

$-1 < x \leq 3$

Practice questions:

Write down the inequality represented on the number lines.

a)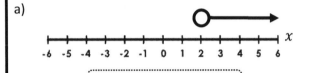

g)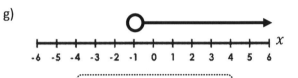

b)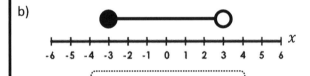

h)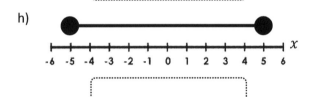

c)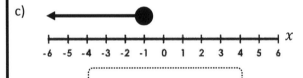

i)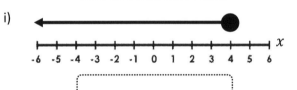

d)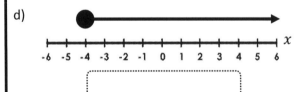

j)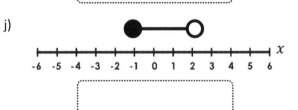

e)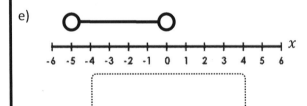

k)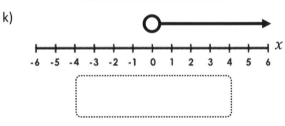

f)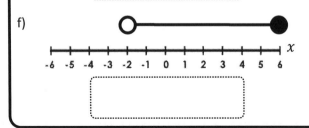

l)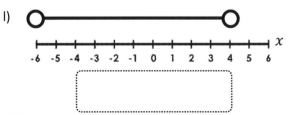

Solve inequalities with one or two variables

Inequalities are solved like normal equations. To do this we need to work backwards using inverses.
If you multiply or divide by a negative number you must flip the inequality.

Examples – one step inequalities

a) Solve: $x + 3 > 7$

$x > 7 - 3$ The inverse of + 3 is − 3

$x > 4$ To get x on its own we need to minus 3 from both sides of the inequality.

b) Solve: $4x \leq 24$

$x \leq 24 \div 4$ The inverse of x 4 is ÷ 4

$x \leq 6$ To get x on its own we need to divide both sides of the inequality by 4.

c) Solve: $-3x < 30$

$x > 30 \div -3$ The inverse of x -3 is ÷ -3

$x > -10$ To get x on its own we need to divide both sides of the inequality by -3.

When dividing by a **negative** number, the inequality *flips* over

Practice questions:

Solve the following inequalities:

a) $x + 1 \geq 2$

b) $x - 3 < 2$

c) $x + 6 \leq 4$

d) $x - 5 \geq -2$

e) $4x > 8$

f) $5x \leq 15$

g) $-2x \geq 6$

h) $6x < -2$

i) $\dfrac{x}{2} > 6$

Examples – two step inequalities

a) Solve: $2x + 5 > 13$

$2x > 13 - 5$ The inverse of + 5 is − 5

$2x > 8$ To get x on its own we need to minus 5 from both sides of the inequality

$x > 4$ To get x on its own we need to divide both sides of the inequality by 2

b) Solve: $-3x - 1 < 17$

$-3x < 17 + 1$ The inverse of - 1 is + 1

$-3x < 18$ To get x on its own we need to add 1 from both sides of the inequality

$x > -6$ To get x on its own we need to divide both sides of the inequality by -3

Practice questions:

Solve the following inequalities:

j) $2x + 7 \geq 11$

k) $3x - 2 < 10$

l) $5x - 3 \leq 42$

m) $9x - 2 \geq 15$

n) $3x + 5 > 29$

o) $-3x + 6 \leq 24$

p) $-4x + 9 \geq 1$

q) $2x + 4 < -8$

r) $\dfrac{x}{-5} + 9 > 4$

Exam question:

Write the first 3 integers in ascending orders that satisfy the inequality $12 < x - 8$

(2)

47

Solve inequalities with one or two variables (2)

Examples – double inequalities

a) Solve: $6 \leq x + 3 < 11$ The inverse of $+ 3$ is $- 3$
       $\mathbf{3 \leq x < 8}$ To get x on its own we need to minus 3 from all parts of the inequality.

b) Solve: $- 8 < 4x \leq 24$ The inverse of x 4 is ÷ 4
       $\mathbf{-2 < x \leq 6}$ To get x on its own we need to divide all parts of the inequality by 4.

c) Solve: $5 \leq 2x - 1 < 31$ Add 1 to all parts of the inequality.
       $6 \leq 2x < 32$ Divide all parts of the inequality by 2.
       $\mathbf{3 \leq x < 16}$

Practice questions:

Solve the following inequalities:

a) $7 < x + 2 < 12$ b) $3 < x - 6 \leq 16$ c) $21 \leq 7x \leq 49$ d) $-3 \leq x + 8 < 7$

e) $22 < 4x + 2 \leq 38$ f) $-9 < 2x - 7 < 13$ g) $-27 \leq 8x + 5 < 69$ h) $-12 \leq 4x - 9 \leq 17$

Example

Represent $x + 3 > 5$ on the number line.

$x > 5 - 3$
$\mathbf{x > 2}$ Plot x > 2 on the number line.

To plot the inequality on the number line you first need to solve it.

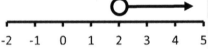

Practice questions:

Plot the inequalities on the number line:

i) $x - 1 < 3$

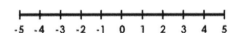

j) $0 < x + 3 \leq 2$

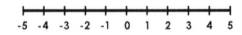

k) $4x \geq -4$

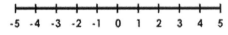

l) $x + 2 \leq -1$

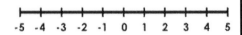

m) $-12 \leq 3x < 6$

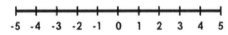

n) $-5x < 10$

o) $-1 \leq 2x - 1 < 5$

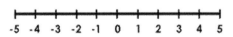

p) $4x - 6 < -18$

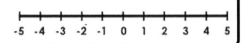

Expanding double brackets

To expand double brackets, you must multiply everything in the first bracket by everything in the second.

Examples

a) Expand and simplify: $(a + 5)(a + 2)$

(i)   (iv)
$(a + 5) (a + 2)$
(ii)
(iii)

Step 1: Multiply each element leaving you with 4 terms.

i) a x a = a^2 ii) 5 x a = 5a   iii) a x 2 = 2a   iv) 5 x 3 = 20

Step 2: Bring the terms together and simplify   = $a^2 + 5a + 2a + 10$ = **$a^2 + 7a + 10$**

Practice questions:
Expand and simplify:

a) $(x + 2)(x + 4)$

e) $(x + 5)(x + 5)$

b) $(x + 5)(x + 3)$

f) $(x + 9)(x + 3)$

c) $(x + 1)(x + 6)$

g) $(3 + x)(x + 3)$

d) $(x + 4)(x + 10)$

h) $(4 + x)(5 + x)$

Examples

a) Expand and simplify: $(x + 5)(x - 2)$ **THE SIGNS MATTER**

(i)   (iv)
$(x + 5) (x - 2)$
(ii)
(iii)

Step 1: Multiply each element leaving you with 4 terms.

i) x x x = x^2 ii) 5 x x = 5x   iii) x x −2 = −2x   iv) 5 x −2 = −10

Step 2: Bring the terms together and simplify   = $x^2 + 5x - 2x - 10$ = **$x^2 + 3x - 10$**

Practice questions:
Expand and simplify:

i) $(x + 2)(x - 4)$

m) $(x + 5)(x - 5)$

j) $(x + 5)(x - 3)$

n) $(x + 9)(x - 3)$

k) $(x - 1)(x + 6)$

o) $(a - 4)(a + 2)$

l) $(x - 5)(x + 1)$

p) $(a - 1)(a + 7)$

Exam question:

The rectangle has two dimensions as shown in the diagram (units are in cm).
Write an expression in the form $x^2 + bx + c$ for its area in cm².

$x + 2$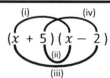

$x + 7$

(2)

Expanding double brackets (2)

Examples:

a) Expand the following: $(a-4)(a-2)$

THE SIGNS MATTER

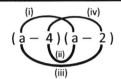

Step 1: Multiply each element leaving you with 4 terms.

i) $a \times a = a^2$ ii) $-4 \times a = -4a$ iii) $a \times -2 = -2a$ iv) $-4 \times -2 = +8$

Step 2: Bring the terms together and simplify. $= a^2 - 4a - 2a + 8$ $= a^2 - 6a + 8$

Practice questions:

Expand and simplify:

a) $(x-2)(x-4)$

e) $(x-5)(x-5)$

b) $(x-5)(x-3)$

f) $(x-3)(x-8)$

c) $(x-1)(x-6)$

g) $(3-x)(3-x)$

d) $(x-4)(x-10)$

h) $(4-x)(5-x)$

Examples

a) Expand and simplify: $(2x+5)(3x-2)$ **THE SIGNS & COEFFICIENTS MATTER**

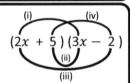

Step 1: Multiply each element leaving you with 4 terms

i) $2x \times 3x = 6x^2$ ii) $5 \times 3x = 15x$ iii) $2x \times -2 = -4x$ iv) $5 \times -2 = -10$

Step 2: Bring the terms together and simplify. $= 6x^2 + 15x - 4x - 10$ $= 6x^2 + 11x - 10$

Practice questions:

Expand and simplify:

i) $(2x+2)(x-4)$

m) $(2x+5)(2x-5)$

j) $(3x+5)(2x-3)$

n) $(3x+9)(x-3)$

k) $(4x-1)(2x+6)$

o) $(3a-4)(4a-2)$

l) $(3x-5)(x+1)$

p) $(2a-3)(3a-2)$

Exam question:

The rectangle has two dimensions as shown in the diagram (units are in cm).

Write an expression for its area in the form $ax^2 + b$.

$2x - 4$

 $3x + 6$

(3)

Factorising quadratics

When factorising quadratics in the form $x^2 + bx + c$, you need to find two numbers which multiply together to get the value of c which also add together to get b. This will then form a double bracket.

Example

a) Solve $x^2 + 5x + 4$

Considering the final number (c) = +4

The factor pairs of +4 are:

2 & 2 , 4 & 1, -2 & -2, -1 & -4

Of these pairs, only 4 and 1 add to make +5 (b)

The factorised answer is therefore $(x + 4)(x + 1)$

b) Solve $x^2 + 2x - 3$

Considering the final number (c) = -3

The factor pairs of -3 are:

1 & -3 , 3 & -1

Of these pairs, only 3 and -1 add to make +2 (b)

The factorised answer is therefore $(x + 3)(x - 1)$

If the quadratic is are in the following forms, then the brackets will look like:

$x^2 + bx + c \rightarrow (x + \ )(x + \ )$

$x^2 - bx + c \rightarrow (x - \ )(x - \ )$

$x^2 - bx - c \rightarrow (x + \ )(x - \ )$

$x^2 + bx - c \rightarrow (x + \ )(x - \ )$

Practice questions: Factorise:

a) $x^2 + 3x + 2$

b) $x^2 + 7x + 10$

c) $x^2 + 8x + 12$

d) $x^2 + 10x + 24$

e) $a^2 + 8a + 7$

f) $x^2 + 10x + 9$

g) $p^2 + 12p + 20$

h) $x^2 + 4x - 5$

i) $y^2 + 2y - 8$

j) $x^2 - 8x + 15$

k) $x^2 + 4x - 21$

l) $x^2 - 4x - 21$

m) $x^2 + 13x + 42$

n) $x^2 - 10x + 25$

o) $k^2 - 5k + 4$

p) $x^2 - x - 30$

q) $x^2 - 2x - 35$

r) $x^2 - 14x + 24$

s) $x^2 - 13x + 42$

t) $e^2 + 11e - 42$

You can check your answer by multiplying out the brackets to get back to the question.

Exam question:

Factorise: $x^2 + xz + xy + yz$

(2)

Solving quadratic equations by factorising

To solve a quadratic equation, it must be in the form $x^2 + bx + c = 0$ where a, b and c are integers.
Sometimes you can solve quadratics by factorising into double brackets.
Once factorised, the solutions are the values which make each bracket equal zero.

Example

Solve $x^2 + 5x + 4 = 0$

Factorising $\rightarrow (x + 4)(x + 1) = 0$

Since anything multiplied by 0 equals 0

Either $x + 4 = 0$ or $x + 1 = 0$

So $x = -4$ or $x = -1$

Solve $x^2 + 2x - 3 = 0$

Factorising $\rightarrow (x - 3)(x + 1) = 0$

Since anything multiplied by 0 equals 0

Either $x - 3 = 0$ or $x + 1 = 0$

So $x = 3$ or $x = -1$

Practice questions: Solve by factorising:

a) $x^2 + 3x + 2 = 0$

b) $x^2 + 7x + 10 = 0$

c) $x^2 + 8x + 12 = 0$

d) $x^2 + 10x + 24 = 0$

e) $x^2 + x - 2 = 0$

f) $x^2 + 3x - 10 = 0$

g) $x^2 + 4x - 21 = 0$

h) $x^2 + 13x + 42 = 0$

i) $x^2 - 10x + 25 = 0$

j) $x^2 - 5x + 4 = 0$

k) $x^2 - x - 30 = 0$

l) $x^2 - 2x - 35 = 0$

Exam question:

Solve $x^2 + 9x = -18$

(3)

Changing the subject of a formula

To change the subject of a formula we need to get a letter on its own. To do this we need to rearrange everything else to the other side of the equation using inverses just like when **solving equations**.

Examples – 1 step

Make y the subject of the formula:

a) $x = y + 4$ To get y on its own – you need to subtract 4 from "both" sides.

    $x - 4 = y$ y is now on its own, so we have made it the subject.   **Answer: $y = x - 4$**

b) $x = \frac{y}{5}$ To get y on its own – you need to multiply "both" sides by 5

    $5x = y$ y is now on it's own, so we have made it the subject.   **Answer: $y = 5x$**

Note: When rearranging a formula, the subject can be on **either** side of the equal side, so the two previous answers can also be written as $y = x - 4$ and $y = 5x$. Cartesian equations often are written as $y = \ldots$

Practice questions:

Make y the subject of the formula:

a) $x = y + 2$

d) $2y = 8x$

g) $x = \frac{y}{7}$

b) $y - 3 = x$

e) $6x = 2y$

h) $\frac{y}{5} = x$

c) $y + 5 = 2x$

f) $4x + 2 = 2y$

i) $x - 1 = \frac{y}{2}$

Example – 2 step

Make d the subject of the formula: $c = 4d + 7$

$c = 4d + 7$ To get d on its own – you first need to subtract 7 from "both" sides

$c - 7 = 4d$ You now need to divide both sides by 4 to get d on it's own.

$\frac{c-7}{4} = d$ d is now on its own, so we have made it the subject.   **Answer : $d = \dfrac{c - 7}{4}$**

Practice questions:

Make y the subject of the formula:

j) $x = 2y + 5$

m) $2y + 4 = 8x$

p) $x = \frac{2y}{7}$

k) $5y - 3 = x$

n) $6x = 2y + 2$

q) $\frac{y}{5} + 2 = x$

l) $4y + 5 = 2x$

o) $4x = \frac{2y}{5}$

r) $x = \frac{y+1}{2}$

Exam question:

The SUVAT equations describe the motion of bodies moving with constant (uniform) acceleration. They are sometimes called the kinematic equations of motion.

This formula represents the relationship between final velocity, initial velocity, acceleration and displacement: $v = u + at$.

Re-arrange the formula to make a the subject.

s is displacement
u is initial velocity
v is final velocity
a is acceleration
t is time

(2)

Changing the subject of a formula with powers

To change the subject of a formula we need to get a letter on its own. To do this we need to rearrange everything else to the other side of the formula using inverses just like when **solving equations**.

Examples : with powers and roots

Make y the subject of the formula:

a) $x = y^2$ To get y on its own you need to take the square root of "both" sides.
  $\sqrt{x} = y$ y is now on its own, so we have made it the subject.

b) $x = \sqrt[3]{y}$ To get y on its own you need to cube "both" sides.
  $x^3 = y$ y is now on it's own, so we have made it the subject.

Note: When rearranging a formula, the subject can be on **either** side of the equal side, so the two previous answers can also be written as $y = \sqrt{x}$ and $y = \sqrt[3]{x}$. Cartesian equations often are written as $y = \ldots$

Practice questions:
Make x the subject of the formula:

a) $y = x^2$

b) $t = x^3$

c) $a = x^5$

d) $\sqrt{x} = y$

e) $\sqrt[4]{x} = w$

f) $u = \sqrt[3]{x}$

Example – two or more steps with powers and roots
Make v the subject of the formula:

a) $r = 5v^2 - 4$ To get v on its own – you need to move the -4 first as it is a separate term.
  $r + 4 = 5v^2$ Now divide by 5 (You leave the power/root until the end).
  $\dfrac{r+4}{5} = v^2$ Finally square root to leave v on its own.
  $\sqrt{\dfrac{r+4}{5}} = v$ When re-arranging, you tend to move values and variables in reverse BIDMAS order.

Practice questions:
Make x the subject of the formula:

g) $y = x^2 + 5$

h) $t = 3x^2$

i) $y = \dfrac{x^2}{4}$

j) $y = x^2 - 9$

k) $y = 2x^2 + 2$

l) $a = bx^2 - 4$

m) $y = \dfrac{x^2}{3} + w$

n) $\dfrac{x^2}{5} = 5y$

o) $y = \dfrac{2}{x^2}$

Exam question:
Re-arrange the formula $s = \frac{1}{2}at^2$ to make $\boldsymbol{t}$ the subject.

(2)

Solving simultaneous equations by elimination

Simultaneous equations can be used to find two unknowns which appear in two different equations. If the equations have a term with the same coefficient and sign, you can subtract one from the other.

Example: Solve the following equations simultaneously (Find the values of x and y).

$5x + 3y = 18$ *(1)* **Step 1:** Label the equations *(1)* and *(2)*.

$3x + 3y = 12$ *(2)* **Step 2:** Since $+3y$ appears in both equations,   → into $3x + 3y = 12$

                     when you subtract *(2)* from *(1)*, $3(3) + 3y = 12$

                     the $3y$ will be eliminated. $9 + 3y = 12$

     $2x = 6$ **Step 3:** Divide by 2. $3y = 3$

     $x = 3$ **Step 4:** Substitute x into one of the equations to find y *(2)*. $y = 1$

Practice questions:

Solve the following simultaneous equations:

a) $5x + 2y = 19$
    $x + 2y = 7$

c) $3x + y = 16$
    $4x + y = 20$

b) $4x + 6y = 34$
    $4x + 3y = 19$

d) $6x + 3y = 33$
    $6x + 8y = 68$

If the coefficients are different in the terms, you need to multiply the equation(s) so that they are the same.

Examples: Solve the following equations simultaneously (Find the values of x and y).

$2x + 2y = 6$ (1) **Step 1:** Label the equations (1) and (2).

$6x + 5y = 16$ (2) **Step 2:** Multiply (1) by 3 to get $6x$ in both equations.   → into $2x + 2y = 6$

$6x + 6y = 18$ (3) **Step 3:** Label new equation as (3). $2x + 2(2) = 6$

                     Step 4: Subtract (2) from (3), $2x + 4 = 6$

                     the $6x$ will be eliminated. $2x = 2$

     $y = 2$ Step 5: Substitute y into one of the equations to find x (1). $x = 1$

Practice questions:

Solve the following simultaneous equations:

e) $2x + 3y = 16$
    $x + 2y = 10$

g) $x + y = 3$
    $5x + 9y = 3$

f) $2x + 2y = 2$
    $8x + 9y = 11$

h) $4x + y = 25$
    $5x + 3y = 40$

Solving simultaneous equations by elimination (2)

> If the equations have a term with the same coefficient and a *different sign*, you can add the two together.

Example: Solve the following equations simultaneously (Find the values of x and y).

$4x + 2y = 16$ *(1)* **Step 1:** Label the equations *(1)* and *(2)*.

$3x - 2y = -2$ *(2)* **Step 2:** $2y$ appear in both equations but the signs are different so add *(1)* and *(2)*, the $2y$ will be eliminated.

         $7x = 14$ **Step 3:** Divide by 7.

         $x = 2$ **Step 4:** Substitute x into one of the equations to find y (1).

into $4x + 2y = 16$
$4(2) + 2y = 16$
$8 + 2y = 16$
$2y = 8$
$\mathbf{y = 4}$

Practice questions:

Solve the following simultaneous equations:

a) $3x + 3y = 21$
    $2x - 3y = -16$

c) $5x - 4y = 35$
    $3x + 4y = 21$

b) $7x + y = 37$
    $x - y = 3$

d) $-2x + 6y = 38$
    $2x + 3y = 16$

> If the coefficients are different in the terms, you need to multiply the equation(s) so that they are the same.

Examples : Solve the following equations simultaneously (Find the values of x and y).

$2x + y = 9$ (1) **Step 1:** Label the equations (1) and (2).

$5x - 4y = 3$ (2) **Step 2:** Multiply (1) by 4 to get $4y$ in both equations.

$8x + 4y = 36$ (3) **Step 3:** Label new equation (3).

                       Step 4: Add (2) and (3), the $4y$ will be eliminated.

        $13x = 39$ **Step 5:** Divide by 13.

        $x = 3$ **Step 5:** Substitute y into one of the equations to find x (1).

into $2x + y = 9$
$2(3) + y = 9$
$6 + y = 9$
$y = 9 - 6$
$\mathbf{y = 3}$

Practice questions:

Solve the following simultaneous equations:

e) $2x + y = 14$
    $6x - 2y = 32$

g) $4x + 7y = 39$
    $-8x + 6y = -58$

f) $2x - 2y = -8$
    $x + 6y = 24$

h) $2x + y = 4$
    $8x - 7y = 60$

If the equations have no coefficients which are the same, then it may be that both equations need to be multiplied to find a common multiple, you can then either add or subtract the two new equations.

Example: Solve the following equations simultaneously (Find the values of x and y).

$3x + 2y = 24$ *(1)* **Step 1:** Label them *(1)* and *(2)*.
$2x + 3y = 21$ *(2)* **Step 2:** Multiply *(1)* by 3 and *(2)* by 2, to get $6y$ in both. $-- \rightarrow$ into $3x + 2y = 24$
$9x + 6y = 72$ *(3)* **Step 3:** Label them *(3)* and *(4)*. $3(6) + 2y = 24$
$4x + 6y = 42$ *(4)* **Step 4:** Subtract *(4)* from *(3)*. $18 + 2y = 24$
$\quad\quad 5x = 30$ **Step 5:** Divide by 5. $2y = 6$
$\quad\quad\quad x = 6$ **Step 6:** Substitute x into one of the equations to find y *(1)*. $y = 3$

Practice questions:

Solve the following simultaneous equations:

a) $6x + 2y = 30$
$\quad 4x + 5y = 53$

e) $5x + 2y = 24$
$\quad 2x - 3y = 2$

b) $7x + 5y = 10$
$\quad 2x + 4y = -10$

f) $4x + 2y = 20$
$\quad 5x - 7y = -51$

c) $7x - 2y = 1$
$\quad 4x - 3y = 8$

g) $4x - 3y = -9$
$\quad 6x + 5y = -23$

d) $7x + 7y = -21$
$\quad 2x + 6y = -14$

h) $7x + 4y = 10$
$\quad 8x - 9y = -70$

Exam question:

Two families go to a theatre production.
The Parker family of two adults and three children pay £69.
The Rogers family of three adults and five children pay £109.
Work out the cost of an adult ticket and a child ticket.

(2)

Solving simultaneous equations by substitution

To solve simultaneous equations by using substitution, you must rearrange one of the equations to make x or y the subject, then substitute it into the other equation, allowing you to solve a linear equation.

Example: Solve the following equations simultaneously (Find the values of x and y).

$y = 4x$ *(1)*   **Step 1:** Label the two equations *(1)* and *(2)*.

$3x + y = 21$ *(2)*   **Step 2:** Substitute *(1)* into *(2)*.

$3x + (4x) = 21$ **Step 3:** Simplify.   into $y = 4x$

$7x = 21$ **Step 4:** Divide by 7. $y = 4(3)$

$x = 3$ **Step 5:** Substitute x into one of the equations to find y *(1)* $y = 12$

Practice questions:

Solve the following simultaneous equations:

a) $y = x + 1$
$4x + y = 21$

c) $y = 3x$
$x + 2y = 21$

b) $y = x$
$3x + 4y = 14$

d) $y = 2x + 3$
$5x + 3y = 20$

Examples: Solve the following equations simultaneously (Find the values of x and y).

$3x + y = 11$ (1)   **Step 1:** Label the two equations (1) and (2).

$7x + 2y = 24$ (2)   **Step 2:** Re-arrange (1) to make y the subject (3).

$y = 11 - 3x$ (3)   **Step 3:** Substitute (3) into (2).   into $y = 11 - 3x$

$7x + 2(11 - 3x) = 24$ **Step 4:** Simplify. $y = 11 - 3(2)$

$7x + 22 - 6x = 24$ **Step 5:** Solve. $y = 5$

$x = 2$ **Step 6:** Substitute x into one of the equations to find y (3).

Practice questions:

Solve the following simultaneous equations:

e) $y = x + 4$
$6x - y = 21$

g) $3x + y = 26$
$2x + 5y = 39$

f) $y = 2x - 5$
$3x - y = 11$

h) $x + 4y = 18$
$7x + 2y = 74$

Algebra in shapes

Knowledge of basic shape properties are often assessed using algebra. You can use your knowledge of shape properties to form expressions and therefore linear equations, in order to solve problems.

Example: Angles in triangles

a) Write an expression for the sum of angles.

Sum of angles: $(x + 5) + (x + 25) + (x)$
= **3x + 30**

b) Hence calculate the value of x.

Angles in a triangle add up to $180°$

Step 1: Form an equation. $3x + 30 = 180$
Step 2: Solve the equation. $3x = 150$
x = 50°

Practice questions:

By forming an equation, calculate the value x:

a)

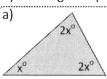

b)

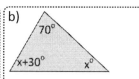

c)

d)

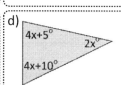

e)

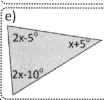

f)

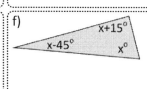

Example: Angles in quadrilaterals

By forming an equation, calculate the value x :

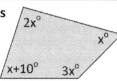

Sum of angles: $(2x) + (x + 10) + (x) + (3x) = 7x + 10$
Angles in a quadrilateral add up to $360°$
Step 1: Form an equation $7x + 10 = 360$
Step 2: Solve the equation. $7x = 350$ **x = 50°**

Practice questions:

Calculate the value of x:

g)

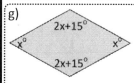

h)

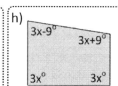

i)

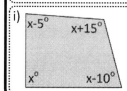

j)

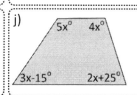

Exam question:

ABC is an isosceles triangle.
$\angle BAC = 2x$, $\angle BCA = 2x$ and $\angle ABC = 40°$.
Find the value of x.

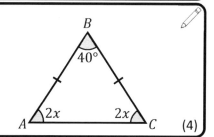

(4)

Algebra in shapes (quadratic equations)

When calculating with shapes and algebra together, you may have to multiply terms together which will result in a quadratic expression or equation being formed. This can then be solved.

Example: Area of shapes

a) Write an expression for the area of the rectangle.

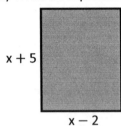

$x + 5$

$x - 2$

Area: $(x + 5)(x-2)$
$= x^2 + 5x - 2x - 10$
$= x^2 + 3x - 10$

b) Hence calculate the value of x if its area is 30cm²

Step 1: Form an equation $x^2 + 3x - 10 = 30$

Step 2: Re-arrange to be in the form $x^2 + bx + c = 0$
$x^2 + 3x - 40 = 0$

Step 3: Factorise $(x + 8)(x - 5) = 0$

Step 4: Solve $x = -8$ or 5

Step 5: Reject $x = -8$ as a length can't be negative

x = 5

Practice questions:

By forming an equation, calculate the value of x:

a) When the area of the rectangle is 21cm²

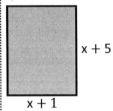

$x + 5$

$x + 1$

b) When the area of the rectangle is 60cm²

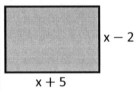

$x - 2$

$x + 5$

c) When the area of the rectangle is 77cm²

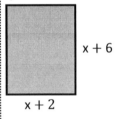

$x + 6$

$x + 2$

d) When the area of the rectangle is 33cm²

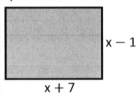

$x - 1$

$x + 7$

e) When the area of the rectangle is 30cm²

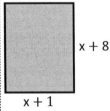

$x + 8$

$x + 1$

f) When the area of the rectangle is 165cm²

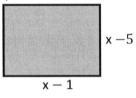

$x - 5$

$x - 1$

Exam question:

The diagram shows a rectangle.
The area of the rectangle is 96cm²
Find the value of x.

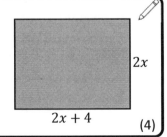

$2x$

$2x + 4$

(4)

The nth term of a sequence

The nth term is used to find any term in a sequence. n represents the term number.
For example, if you want to find the 7th term, you would substitute the value of 7 for n in the nth term.

Example:

a) Given that the nth term of a sequence is **7n**

Find the i) 1st term $7(1) = $ **7**

      ii) 5th term $7(5) = $ **35**

      iii) 9th term $7(9) = $ **45**

b) Given that the nth term of a sequence is = **4n − 2**

Find the i) 1st term $4(1) - 2 = $ **2**

      ii) 3rd term $4(3) - 2 = $ **10**

      iii) 7th term $4(7) - 2 = $ **26**

Practice questions:

Find the 1st, 3rd, 5th and 100th terms of the following sequences:

	1st Term	3rd Term	5th Term	100th Term
a) n + 4				
b) 3n				
c) 2n + 5				
d) 3n − 2				
e) 3 − 4n				
f) − 5n − 7				

When substituting into a quadratic n^{th} term, ensure you use brackets as you are less likely to make a mistake. Powers must go on the outside of the brackets ( )²

Example:

a) **The nth term of a sequence is given as $n^2 + 4n + 6$**

Find the i) 1st term $(1)^2 + 4(1) + 6 = $ **11**

      ii) 5th term $(5)^2 + 4(5) + 6 = $ **51**

      iii) 9th term $(9)^2 + 4(9) + 6 = $ **123**

b) The nth term of a sequence is given as $2n^2 − 3n$

Find the i) 1st term $2(1)^2 − 3(1) = $ **−1**

      ii) 3rd term $2(3)^2 − 3(3) = $ **9**

      iii) 7th term $2(7)^2 − 3(7) = $ **77**

Practice questions:

Find the 1st, 3rd, 5th and 100th terms of the following sequences

	1st Term	3rd Term	5th Term	10th Term
g) $n^2 + 3$				
h) $2n^2$				
i) $n^2 + 3n$				
j) $n^2 − 2n$				
k) $n^2 − 3n + 1$				
l) $2n^2 + 3n − 7$				

Exam question:

The nth term of a sequence is: $2n^2 + 4n − 1$

Work out the 10th term of the sequence

(2)

The nth term of a sequence (2)

To generate a sequence using the nth term, you must substitute n = 1, n = 2, n = 3, n = 4 and n = 5 to get the first 5 terms.

Example:
a) Given that the nth term of a sequence is **5n + 2**, write down the first 5 terms of the sequence

Find the 1st term (n = 1)   5(1) + 2 = **7**   4th term (n = 4)   5(4) + 2 = **22**

2nd term (n = 2)   5(2) + 2 = **12**   5th term (n = 5)   5(5) + 2 = **27**

3rd term (n = 3)   5(3) + 2 = **17**

First 5 terms: **7, 12, 17, 22, 27**

Practice questions:
Find the first 5 terms of the following sequences:

a) 8n + 4

b) 3n − 4

c) 25 − 6n

d) $3n^2$

e) $n^2 + 4n − 3$

f) $5n^2 − 7n$

To find the nth term you firstly need to find the difference between the terms, this number goes in front of n. You then need to see what you have to add or subtract to get to the sequence.

Example:
a) Find the nth term of the sequence:
   4, 7, 10, 13, 16…

The sequence is going up in 3's so the first part of the nth term is 3n. 3n is the same as the 3 times table which gives: 3, 6, 9, 12, 15… We need to add 1 onto all of the terms to get to the original sequence. **nth term = 3n + 1**

b) Find the nth term of the sequence:
   1, 7, 13, 19, 25…

The sequence is going up in 6's so the first part of the nth term is 6n. 6n is the same as the 6 times table which gives: 6, 12, 18, 24, 30… We need to subtract 5 from all of the terms to get to the original sequence. **nth term = 6n - 5**

Practice questions:
Find the nth term of the sequences:

g) 3, 5, 7, 9, 11 …

h) 2, 6, 10, 14, 18…

i) 7, 12, 17, 22, 27…

j) 0, 4, 8, 12, 16…

k) 1, 9, 17, 25, 33…

l) 4, 10, 16, 22, 28…

m) 2, 14, 26, 38, 50…

n) -8, -3, 2, 7, 12…

o) 16, 14, 12, 10, 8…

p) 2, -3, -8, -13, -18…

Exam question:
Here are the first five terms of a number sequence. 7, 10, 13, 16, 19
a) Write an expression, in terms of n, for the nth term of this number sequence.

b) Find the 85th term in this number sequence.

(3)

Is a number in a sequence?

To find if a number is in a sequence you can find the nth term and set it equal to the number. If you then solve the equation it will give you the term number which corresponds to the given number. If the term number is an integer then it is in the sequence, if it is a decimal it is not in the sequence.

Example:

a) A sequence is given by: 6, 13, 20, 27...
   Is 104 a term in the sequence?

The nth term of the sequence is: $7n - 1$
Form and solve an equation: $7n - 1 = 104$ (+1)
$$7n = 105 \quad (\div 7)$$
$$n = 15$$
This means 104 is the 15th term of the sequence.
Yes, 104 is a term in the sequence.

b) A sequence is given by: 12, 21, 30, 39...
   Is 234 a term in the sequence?

The nth term of the sequence is: $9n + 3$
Form and solve an equation: $9n + 3 = 234$ (-3)
$$9n = 231 \quad (\div 9)$$
$$n = 25.67$$
This means 234 is the 26.67^{th} term of the sequence. This doesn't make sense as a term must be a whole number. **No, 234 is not a term in the sequence.**

Practice questions:

a) 4, 7, 10, 13... is 250 in the sequence?

b) 14, 20, 26, 32... is 148 in the sequence?

c) 15, 19, 23, 27... is 371 in the sequence?

d) 1, 9, 17, 25... is 229 in the sequence?

e) 3, 14, 25, 36... is 444 in the sequence?

f) 8, 15, 22, 29... is 519 in the sequence?

g) 18, 31, 44, 59... is 600 in the sequence?

h) 12, 31, 50, 69... is 778 in the sequence?

i) 320, 314, 308, 302... is 50 in the sequence?

j) 870, 861, 852, 843... is 77 in the sequence?

Find the midpoint of a straight line

A midpoint of a line is the co-ordinate exactly in the middle of the line.

Example:

Find the midpoints of the line shown

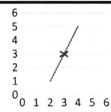

You may be able to see where the midpoint is
You can also count half way up, and half way across. Midpoint = **(3, 3)**

Practice questions:

Write the co-ordinate of the midpoints of the lines shown

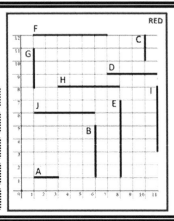

RED

A) (___ , ___) F) (___ , ___)

B) (___ , ___) G) (___ , ___)

C) (___ , ___) H) (___ , ___)

D) (___ , ___) I) (___ , ___)

E) (___ , ___) J) (___ , ___)

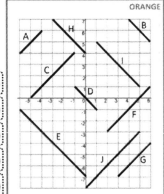

ORANGE

A) (___ , ___) F) (___ , ___)

B) (___ , ___) G) (___ , ___)

C) (___ , ___) H) (___ , ___)

D) (___ , ___) I) (___ , ___)

E) (___ , ___) J) (___ , ___)

Another way to find the midpoint is by finding the mean of the two co-ordinates. If a line has endpoints (x_1, y_1) and (x_2, y_2) then:

$$\text{Midpoint} = \left(\frac{x_1 + x_2}{2}, \frac{y_1 + y_2}{2}\right)$$

Example

Find the midpoints of the line that join the points (2, 3) and (4, 11)

$x_1 = 2 \quad y_1 = 3 \quad x_2 = 4 \quad y_2 = 11$
$\left(\dfrac{x_1 + x_2}{2}, \dfrac{y_1 + y_2}{2}\right) = \left(\dfrac{2 + 4}{2}, \dfrac{3 + 11}{2}\right) = \left(\dfrac{6}{2}, \dfrac{14}{2}\right) = (3, 7)$

TIP. Be careful when using negatives, and if using algebra – the techniques given are the same

Practice questions:

Find the midpoint of the line with the following endpoints:

a) $(0, 1)$ and $(4, 9)$

b) $(5, 0)$ and $(5, 2)$

c) $(8, 5)$ and $(14, 17)$

d) $(2, 0)$ and $(8, 5)$

e) $(4, 3)$ and $(11, 8)$

f) $(4, 4)$ and $(1, 27)$

g) $(-1, 8)$ and $(-5, -2)$

h) $(-5, -7)$ and $(-1, 1)$

i) $(-2, -6)$ and $(-10, 0)$

j) $(-9, -2)$ and $(-5, -16)$

k) $(-5, 6)$ and $(2, -1)$

l) $(0, -4)$ and $(9, -9)$

Exam question:

AB is a straight line such that M is the midpoint of the line AB.

A is at $(3x, 2y)$ and B is at $(7x, 6y)$.

Find the co-ordinates of M in terms of x and y.

(2)

Horizontal and vertical lines

A horizontal line cuts through the y-axis.
The equation of a horizontal line is always in the form y = a, a is the point where the line crosses the y-axis.

A vertical line cuts through the x-axis.
The equation of a vertical line is always in the form x = a, a is the point where the line crosses the x-axis.

Example:
Write down the equations of the lines:

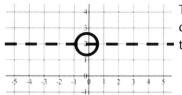

This is a horizontal line cutting through 2 on the y-axis

$$y = 2$$

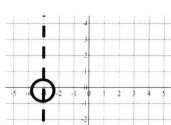

This is a vertical line cutting through -3 on the x-axis

$$x = -3$$

Practice questions:
Write down the equations of the lines;

a)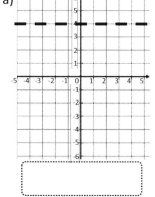

b)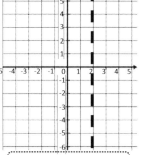

c)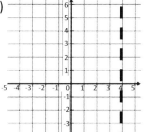

d)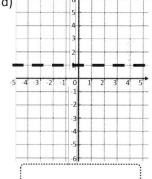

e)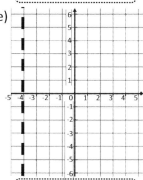

f)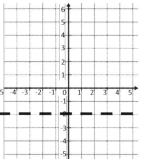

g)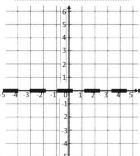

h)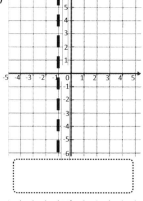

i)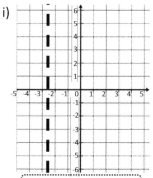

j)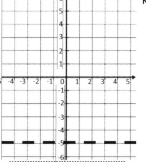

k)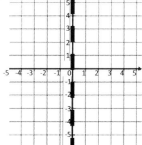

l)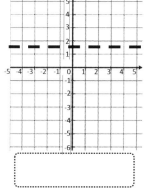

The equation of a line: y-intercept (c)

Every straight line graph has an equation which can be written in the form y = mx + c.
c is the y-intercept (the value where the line crosses the y-axis).

Example:

Find the value of c (y-intercept) of the following lines:

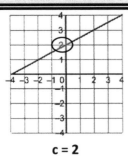

c = 2

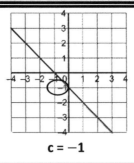

c = −1

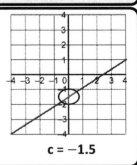

c = −1.5

Practice questions:

Write down the y-intercept of the following lines:

a)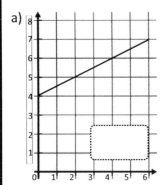

b)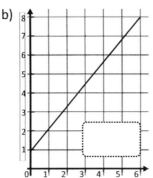

c)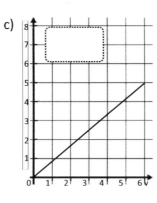

d)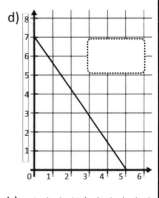

e)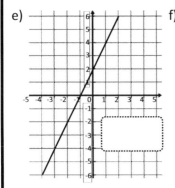

f)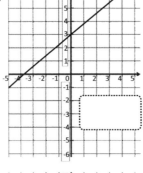

g)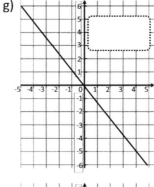

h)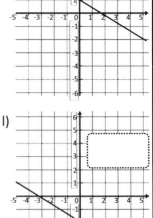

i)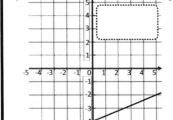

j)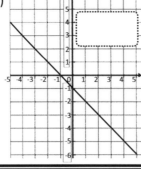

k)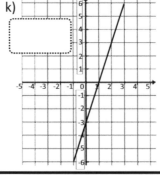

l)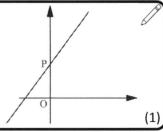

Exam question:

The line $y = 2x + 4$ crosses the y axis at P.
What is the value of y at P?

(1)

The equation of a line: gradient (m)

Every straight line graph has an equation which can be written in the form y = mx + c.
m is the gradient of the line (this is sometimes called the slope, and indicates the steepness of the line.
To find the gradient: Pick 2 points on the line, join them to make a right angled triangle and then calculate:
the **increase in the vertical** ÷ the **increase in the horizontal.**

Example:

a) Find the gradient
   of the line

$$\frac{increase\ in\ y}{increase\ in\ x} = \frac{8}{4}$$

Gradient = 2

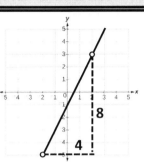

$$Gradient\ (m) = \frac{increase\ in\ y}{increase\ in\ x}$$

b) Find the gradient
   of the line

$$\frac{increase\ in\ y}{increase\ in\ x} = \frac{-8}{6}$$

Gradient $= -\frac{4}{3}$

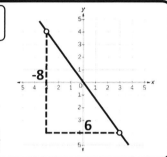

Practice questions:

Find the gradient of the following lines:

a)
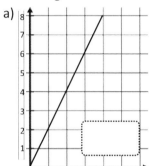

b)
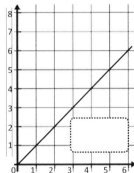

c)
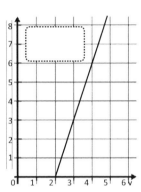

d)
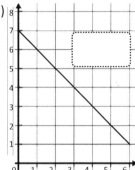

e)
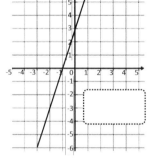

f)
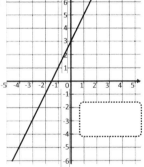

g)
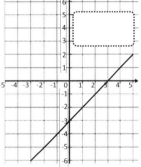

h)
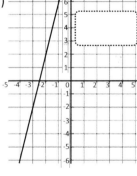

i)
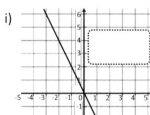

j)
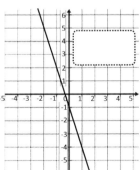

k)
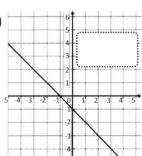

l)
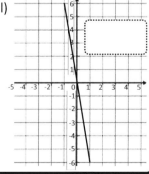

Exam question:

The line $y = 2x + 3$ crosses the y axis at P.
What is the gradient of the line?

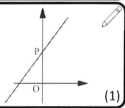

(1)

67

The equation of a line: $y = mx + c$

Every straight line graph has an equation which can be written in the form y = mx + c.
To write the equation in this format, you need to identify both the y-intercept (c) and the gradient (m).

Example:

a) Find the equation
   of this line ⟶

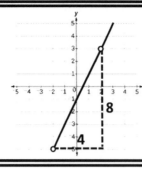

Gradient (m) = 2
y-intercept (c) = −1

Equation is: **y = 2x−1**

Equation in form $y = mx + c$

b) Find the equation
   of this line ⟶

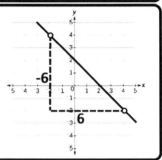

Gradient (m) = −1
y-intercept (c) = 2

Equation is **y = −x + 2**

Practice questions:

Write down the equation of the following lines in the form $y = mx + c$:

a)
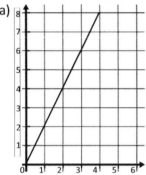

b)
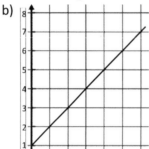

c)
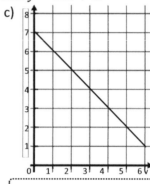

d)
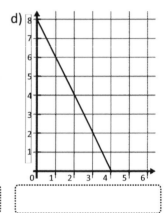

e)
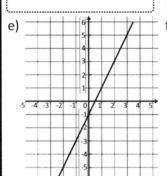

f)
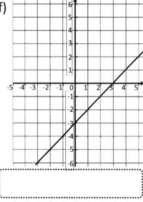

g)
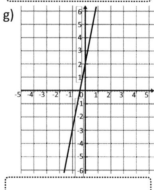

h)
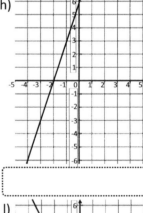

i)
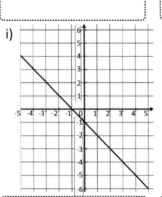

j)
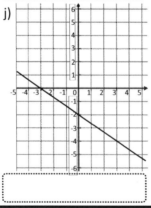

k)
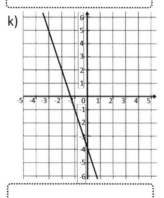

l)
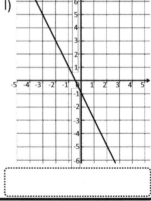

Exam question:

A straight line has a gradient of 4
and crosses the y-axis at (0, -3).

Write the equation of the line in the form $y = ax + b$ where a and b are integer values. (2)

The equation of a line: $y = mx + c$ (2)

Every straight line graph has an equation which can be written in the form $y = mx + c$, where m is the gradient and c is the y-intercept. When asked for the co-ordinate of the y intercept you must give it as (0, c).

Example:

a) Write down the gradient and co-ordinate of the y-intercept of the line: $y = 5x + 7$

Comparing $y = 5x + 7$ to $y = mx + c$ the gradient is the number in front of x so the **gradient = 5**

The y-intercept is the number on it's own so the y-intercept is 7. **Co-ordinate of the y-intercept = (0, 7)**

b) Write down the gradient and co-ordinate of the y-intercept of the line: $y = 6 - 3x$

Comparing $y = 6 - 3x$ to $y = mx + c$ the gradient is the number in front of x so the **gradient = -3**

The y-intercept is the number on it's own so the y-intercept is 6. **Co-ordinate of the y-intercept = (0, 6)**

Practice questions:

Write down the gradient and co-ordinate of the y intercept of the following lines:

a) $y = 7x + 2$

Gradient =

y-intercept: (,   )

b) $y = 5x + 4$

Gradient =

y-intercept: (,   )

c) $y = \frac{1}{2}x - 6$

Gradient =

y-intercept: (,   )

d) $y = x + 9$

Gradient =

y-intercept: (,   )

e) $y = 3x$

Gradient =

y-intercept: (,   )

f) $y = -4x + 7$

Gradient =

y-intercept: (,   )

g) $y = -8x - 1$

Gradient =

y-intercept: (,   )

h) $y = 9 - 3x$

Gradient =

y-intercept: (,   )

i) $y = -11 - x$

Gradient =

y-intercept: (,   )

Example:

Write down the equation of the line with gradient 7 passing through the point (0, -4)

As the co-ordinate is in the form (0, c)   c = -4   m = 7   using $y = mx + c$ $y = 7x - 4$

Practice questions:

Write down the equation of the line:

j) Gradient = 4
passing through (0, 3)

k) Gradient = 8
passing through (0, 9)

l) Gradient = -2
passing through (0, 6)

m) Gradient = 1
passing through (0, -7)

n) Gradient = 9
passing through (0, -3)

o) Gradient = -6
passing through (0, -4)

p) Gradient = -1
passing through (0, 6)

q) Gradient = 3
passing through (0, 0)

Drawing straight line graphs

When drawing straight line graphs, you need to fill in a table of values.
These values are then used as co-ordinates which you can plot and join up. If you are not given a table of values, you can pick your own x values to calculate the y values (pick 3 or more).

Example:

Plot $y = 2x + 2$

x	0	1	2	3
y	2	4	6	8

Step 1: Draw a table of values and pick the x values.

Step 2: Sub the x values into $y = 2x + 2$ to find the y values.

When $x = 0 \rightarrow 2(0) + 2 = 2$ (0,2)
When $x = 1 \rightarrow 2(1) + 2 = 4$ (1,4)
When $x = 2 \rightarrow 2(2) + 2 = 6$ (2,6)
When $x = 3 \rightarrow 2(3) + 2 = 8$ (3,8)

Step 3: Plot the co-ordinates.

Step 4: Join with a straight line.

Make sure you draw the line all the way along your graph!

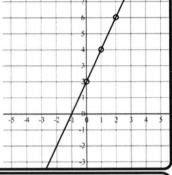

Practice questions:

Complete the table of values and then plot the following straight line graphs for the given equations:

a) $y = x + 4$

x	−1	0	1	2
y				

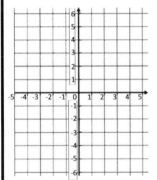

b) $y = 2x$

x	−1	0	1	2
y				

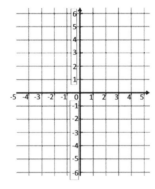

c) $y = x - 3$

x	0	1	2	3
y				

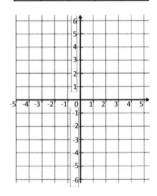

d) $y = 2x + 1$

x	−2	−1	0	2
y				

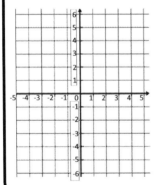

e) $y = 2x - 2$

x	−1	0	1	2
y				

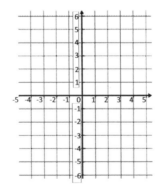

f) $y = 5 - x$

x	1	2	3	4
y				

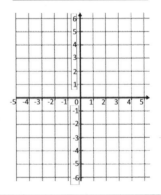

Exam question:

A straight line is given by the equation $y = 4x - 3$.

Complete the table of values given for the values of y for the x values in the table.

x	−2	−1	0	1	2	3
y						

(2)

Drawing quadratic graphs

When drawing quadratic graphs, you will need to fill in a table of values.
These values are then used as co-ordinates, which you plot to support you in drawing the graph.

Example:

Plot $y = x^2 + x - 4$

Step 1: A table of values

x	-3	-2	-1	0	1	2	3
y	2	-2	-4	-4	-2	2	8

Use brackets to avoid negative errors: $(-3)^2 = 9$

Step 2: Sub the x values into $y = x^2 + x - 4$ to find the y values

When $x = -3 \rightarrow (-3)^2 + (-3) - 4 = 2$ $(-3, 2)$

When $x = -2 \rightarrow (-2)^2 + (-2) - 4 = -2$ $(-2, -2)$

When $x = -1 \rightarrow (-1)^2 + (-1) - 4 = -4$ $(-1, -4)$

When $x = 0 \rightarrow (0)^2 + (0) - 4 = -4$ $(0, -4)$

When $x = 1 \rightarrow (1)^2 + (1) - 4 = -2$ $(1, -2)$

When $x = 2 \rightarrow (2)^2 + (2) - 4 = 2$ $(2, 2)$

When $x = 3 \rightarrow (3)^2 + (3) - 4 = 8$ $(3, 8)$

Step 3: Plot the co-ordinates which **will** form a "parabola"

Step 4: Join with a curved line through the points

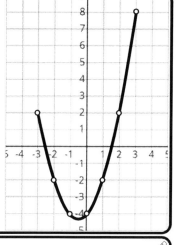

Practice questions:

Use the table of values to help you plot the following graphs:

a) $y = x^2 + 1$

b) $y = x^2 + x$

c) $y = x^2 + 4x + 1$

d) $y = x^2 - x - 5$

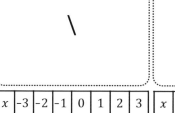

x	-3	-2	-1	0	1	2	3
y							

x	-3	-2	-1	0	1	2	3
y							

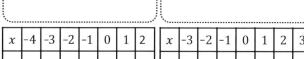

x	-4	-3	-2	-1	0	1	2
y							

x	-3	-2	-1	0	1	2	3
y							

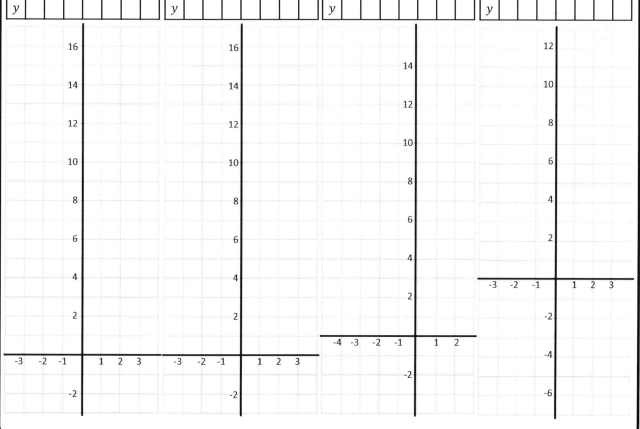

Inequalities on graphs

To sketch an inequality on a graph you must first draw the line which represents the inequality as if it were an equation with an equal sign, and then shade the side of the line which the inequality represents.
If the inequality is 'equal to' ($\leq$ or $\geq$) you must use a solid line. ─────
If the inequality is ' not equal to' you must use a dashed line. ─ ─ ─ ─ ─

Example: Shade the region which represents $x + y < 3$

Step 1: Draw the line $x + y = 3$
Step 2: You must use a dashed line because $y > x + 1$ is not 'or equal to'.
Step 3: Check a point on one side of the line (2, 4)
Step 4: Sub (2, 4) into $x + y < 3$ → $2 + 4 < 3$ → $6 < 3$ which is <u>not true</u>
so this point is in the incorrect section.
Step 5: Shade the section which satisfies the inequality.

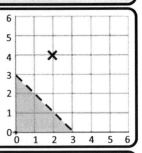

Practice questions:

Shade the regions which satisfy the given inequalities on the graphs provided

a) $x \geq 3$

b) $y < 5$

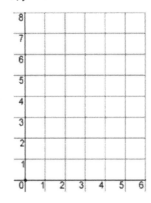

c) $y \geq 4$

d) $x > 2$

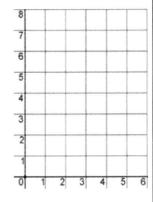

e) $y \leq x$

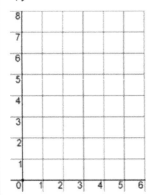

f) $y < 2x$

g) $y + x > 5$

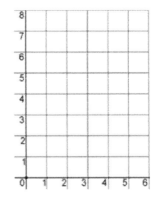

h) $x + y \leq 4$

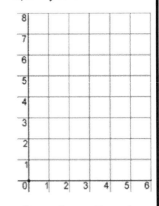

i) $x < 4$ and
$\quad y \leq x$

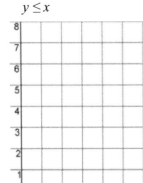

j) $y + x > 6$ and
$\quad y > 5$

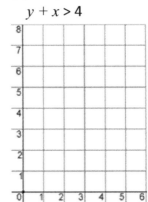

k) $y \leq x$, $x < 5$ and
$\quad y + x > 4$

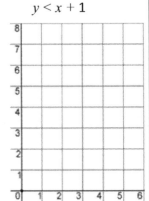

l) $y \geq 3$, $x \leq 5$ and
$\quad y < x + 1$

Conversion Graphs

Conversion graphs are used to change between two different units.

Example:

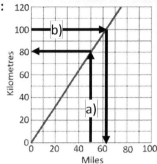

This is a conversion graph between miles and kilometres.

a) Convert 50 miles to kilometres.
  Step 1: Find 50 on the miles axis (x).
  Step 2: Draw a straight line up towards the line.
  Step 3: Draw a straight line across to km axis (y).
  Step 4: Read the value.   **80 km**

b) Convert 100km to miles.
  Read the graph in the opposite direction   **62 miles**
  when converting the other way around.

Practice questions:

Use the conversion graph shown to convert:

a) £40 to pesos

e) £18 to pesos

b) £10 to pesos

f) ₱750 to pounds

c) ₱500 to pounds

g) ₱550 to pounds

d) ₱300 to pounds

h) £34 to pesos

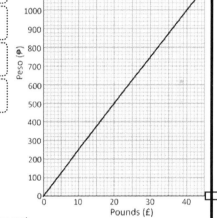

Use the conversion graph shown to convert:

i) $40 to pounds

m) £15 to dollars

j) £40 to dollars

n) $50 to pounds

k) £5 to dollars

o) £50 to dollars

l) $45 to pounds

p) $100 to pounds

Use the conversion graphs shown to convert:

Hint : Convert to pounds first

r) $20 to pesos

s) ₱400 to dollars

Exam question:

The graphs show the conversion between litres and fluid ounces.

a) Convert 4 litres to fluid ounces.

b) Convert 60 fluid ounces to litres.

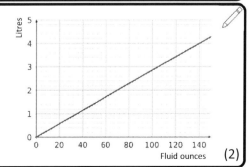

(2)

73

Angles in parallel lines

Vertically opposite angles
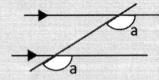
When two straight lines cross (make an X shape), the angles on the opposite sides are equal. These are called 'vertically opposite' angles.

Corresponding angles
When a line crosses two parallel lines and make an F shape, the angles are equal. These are called 'corresponding' angles.

Alternate angles
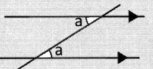
When a line crosses two parallel lines and make a Z shape, the angles are equal. These are called 'alternate' angles.

Co-interior angles
When a line crosses two parallel lines and make a C shape, the inside angles add up to 180°. These are called 'co-interior' angles.
(sometimes referred to as supplementary angles)

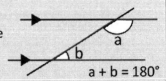
$a + b = 180°$

Examples:

a) Find the missing angle (x).

151° and x are co-interior so sum to 180°
x = 180 − 151 = **29°**

b) Find the missing angle (x).

51 and x are corresponding angles so are equal
x = 51°

Practice questions:

Calculate the missing angle x and state the reason for your answer:

a)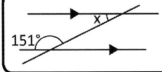

b)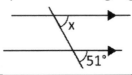

c)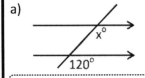

d)

e)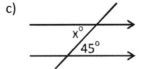

f)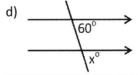

g)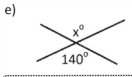

h)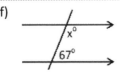

i)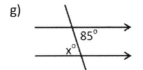

j)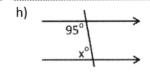

k)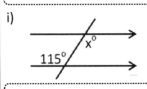

l)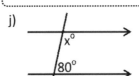

Exam question:

The diagram shows two parallel lines and a triangle ABC.
Find the value of angle ABC.
You must state the reason for your answer.

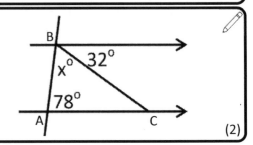

(2)

74

Interior and exterior angles

The interior angles are the angles inside a polygon.
The exterior angles are those between the shape and an extended side.

Corresponding Interior and exterior angles add up to 180°
because they make a straight line.

Exterior angle
Interior angle

Example:

The interior angles of a regular polygon are 62°.
Find the exterior angles

Since interior and exterior angles add to make 180°:
Exterior angle = 180 − 62 = **118°**

Practice questions:

Calculate the corresponding exterior angle if the interior angle is:

a) 75°

b) 95°

c) 60°

d) 45°

e) 125°

f) 169°

g) 70.5°

h) 68.5°

i) 52.3°

The **exterior** angles in any polygon add up to 360° because they make a full 'turn'.

A+B+C+D = 360°

You can calculate the exterior angle of any **regular** polygon by dividing 360° by the number of sides.

Example:

Calculate the exterior and interior angles of a regular pentagon.

Number of sides of a pentagon: 5
Exterior angle = 360 ÷ 5 = **72°**   (as regular)
Interior angle = 180 − 72 = **108°**   (forms a straight line)

Practice questions:

Calculate the size of each interior and exterior angle of the **regular** shapes:

j)

k)

l)

m)

Interior	Exterior	Interior	Exterior	Interior	Exterior	Interior	Exterior

n) Decagon

o) Octagon

p) Hexagon

q) 18 sided shape

Interior	Exterior	Interior	Exterior	Interior	Exterior	Interior	Exterior

Exam question: **Not** drawn accurately

Find the number of sides of a
regular polygon which has
an exterior angle of 30°.

30°

(2)

Angles in polygons

Any polygon can be split into triangles to find the sum of the interior angles.

 If you pick a vertex (corner) and draw lines to the other vertices from your chosen point, it will create a number of triangles. If you multiply the number of triangles by 180° (angles in a triangle), this will give you the sum of interior angles of the polygon In the diagram shown: 3 x 180° = 540°.

There are 2 fewer triangles than sides: **Sum of angles = (n − 2) x 180**, (where *n* is the number of sides).

Example:

What is the sum of the interior angles of an 11 sided polygon?

Use the formula: (*n* – 2) x 180 where n = 11
Sum of angles = (11 – 2) x 180
= 9 x 180 = **1620°**

Practice questions:

Calculate the sum of interior angles for the following shapes:

a)

b)

c)

d)

e) Hexagon

f) Octagon

g) 15 sided shape

h) 102 sided shape

You can calculate the interior angle of any **regular** polygon by dividing the sum of the interior angles by the number of sides. A square is a regular quadrilateral, so each angle is the sum (360°) divide by 4 (90°).

Example:

What is the interior angle of a regular hexagon?

A Hexagon has 6 sides.
Step 1: Sum of angles = (6 – 2) x 180 = 4 x 180 = 720°
Step 2: Divide the sum by number of sides, 720 ÷ 6 = **120°**

Practice questions:

Calculate the size of each interior angle of the **regular** shapes:

i) Pentagon

j) Decagon

k) Nonagon

l) Heptagon

m) 40 sided shape

n) 12 sided shape

o) 72 sided shape

p) 105 sided shape

Exam question:

The diagram shows part of a **regular** 11-sided polygon.
Work out the size of the angle marked *x*.

Not drawn accurately

(2)

Missing angles in a polygon

To calculate a missing angle in a polygon you first need to calculate the sum of all the internal angles. You can then subtract the total of the known angles away from the angle sum to find the missing angle.

Example

Find the size of angle x.

First find the sum of the angles: (6 – 2) x 180 = 720°

Subtract the known angles from the sum:

x = 720 – (105 + 105 + 160 + 100 + 135) = **115°**

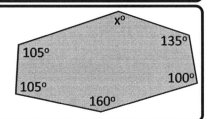

Practice questions:

Find the size of the angle x.

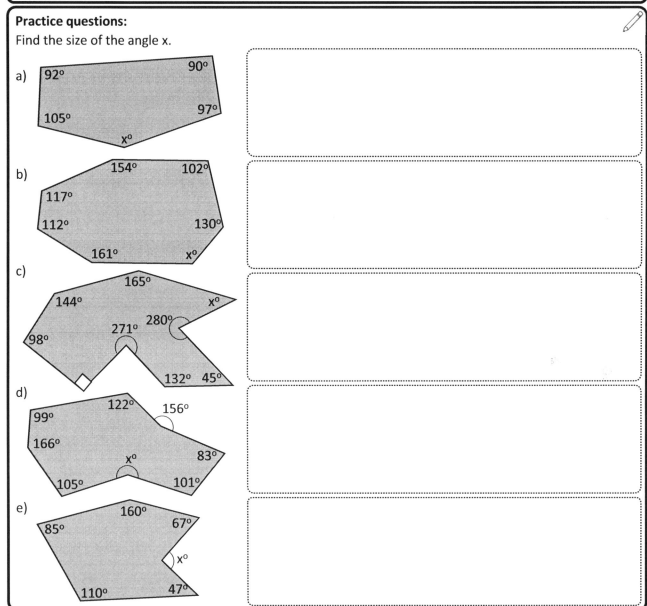

a) 92°   90°   105°   97°   x°

b) 154°   102°   117°   112°   130°   161°   x°

c) 165°   144°   x°   280°   98°   271°   132°   45°

d) 122°   156°   99°   166°   x°   83°   105°   101°

e) 160°   85°   67°   x°   110°   47°

Exam question:

The diagram shows the pentagon ABCDE.
Angle CDE is twice as big as angle BCD.
Calculate the size of angle CDE.

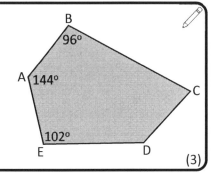

A 144°   B 96°   C   102° E   D

(3)

Bearings

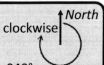

Bearings are used to specify a direction
The angle starts at North and moves around in a clockwise direction
They are called three figure bearings because they are always given as 3 figures long
If the angle is less than 100° you must put a zero in front. e.g. 40° as a three figure bearing is 040°

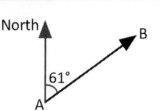

Example:
To find the bearing of A to B *(or the bearing of B from A)*

Step 1: Draw in the North line
Step 2: In a **clockwise** direction, measure the angle between the North line and the line towards B.
Step 3: Write the value as three figure bearing = **061°**

Practice questions:
Write the 3 figure bearings of y from in the following diagrams

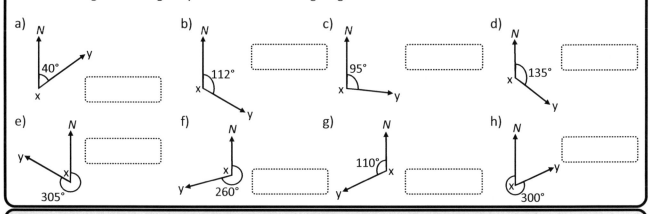

a)

40°

b)

112°

c)

95°

d)

135°

e)

305°

f)

260°

g)

110°

h)

300°

When considering bearings, because lines refer to "north", questions may require you to incorporate other angles theories such as 'angles in parallel' lines, as the north lines are parallel.

Example:
Find the bearing of A from B if the bearing of B from A is 80°

Step 1: Draw in the North lines
Step 2: Since co-interior angles in parallel lines and up to 180° → 180 − 80 = 100°
Step 3: Angle at B going clockwise must therefore be 360 − 100 = **260°**

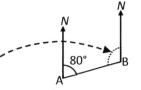

Practice questions:
Write the 3 figure bearings of A to B in the following diagrams

i)

B

230°

A

j)

A

B 310°

k)

85°

A

B

l)

A

B

Exam question:
The bearing of Tree A from Tree B is 060°
Calculate the bearing of Tree B from Tree A

(2)

Compound measures – speed

A compound measure is calculated using two other measurements. Speed is a compound measure because it is calculated with distance and time. The units of speed depend on the units of distance and time, common units are mph, km/h and m/s.

$$\text{Speed} = \frac{\text{Distance}}{\text{Time}}$$

$$\text{Time} = \frac{\text{Distance}}{\text{Speed}}$$

$$\text{Distance} = \text{Speed} \times \text{Time}$$

Example:
A car travels 60 miles in 3 hours.
Calculate its average speed.

Step 1 : Identify the correct formula (using the triangle: S = D ÷ T).
Step 2 : Input the numbers being careful of units
Speed = 60 ÷ 3 = **20 mph**

Practice questions:
Calculate the speed of a vehicle if:

Clearly state the units of your answer

a) It travels 30 metres in 5 seconds.

b) It travels 24km in 4 hours.

c) It travels 72 miles in 9 hours.

d) It travels 120 metres in 15 seconds.

e) It travels 3 km in 60 minutes.

Practice questions:
Calculate the distance travelled if a vehicle:

Clearly state the units of your answer

f) Travels at 9 m/s for 3 seconds.

g) Travels at 50 mph for 10 hours.

h) Travels at 24 km/h for 11 ½ hours.

i) Travels at 13 m/s for 4 hours.

j) Travels at 40 km/h for 38 seconds.

Practice questions:
Calculate the time a vehicle takes to travel:

Clearly state the units of your answer

k) 330 metres, going at 15 m/s.

l) 72 metres, going at 4 m/s.

m) 48 kilometres, going at 6 km/h.

n) 8 kilometres, going at 40 m/s.

o) 900 metres, going at 3 km/h.

Exam question:
An aeroplane is travels at a speed 650 km/hour.
If the flight time between two destinations is 8hrs and 15 minutes.
How far apart to the nearest 100km are the two destinations?

(2)

Compound measures – density

Density tells you how compact an object it is. Density is a compound measure because it is calculated with mass & volume. Common units of density are g/cm^3 and kg/m^3.

$$Density = \frac{Mass}{Volume}$$

$$Volume = \frac{Mass}{Density}$$

$$Mass = Density \times Volume$$

Example:

Calculate the density of an object with mass 84g and volume of $5cm^3$.

Step 1 : Identify the correct formula (using the triangle: $D = M \div V$).

Step 2 : Input the numbers being careful of units.

Density = $84 \div 5$ = **16.8 g/cm^3**

Practice questions:

Calculate the density of an object:

Clearly state the units of your answer

a) With a mass of 18g and volume $6cm^3$

b) With a mass of 56kg and volume $7m^3$

c) With a mass of 108g and volume $12cm^3$

d) With a mass of 3kg and volume $200cm^3$

e) With a mass of 4200g and volume $2.1m^3$

Practice questions:

Calculate the mass of an object:

Clearly state the units of your answer

f) With a volume of $2cm^3$ and density $8g/cm^3$

g) With a volume of $8m^3$ and density $12kg/m^3$

h) With a volume of $9cm^3$ and density $30g/cm^3$

i) With a volume of $40cm^3$ and density $16g/cm^3$

j) With a volume of $8m^3$ and density $5.6kg/m^3$

Practice questions:

Calculate the volume of an object:

Clearly state the units of your answer

k) With a mass of 20kg and density $5kg/cm^3$

l) With a mass of 30g and density $4g/cm^3$

m) With a mass of 107kg and density $10kg/m^3$

n) With a mass of 1200g and density $4kg/m^3$

o) With a mass of 80kg and density $16g/cm^3$

Exam question:

Brass has a density of has $8.1g/cm^3$.

If the volume of a brass door knob is $133.65 \ cm^3$

Find the mass of the brass door knob.

Give your answer to the nearest gram.

(2)

Compound measures – pressure

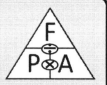

Pressure is the force applied to a surface by an object. Pressure is a compound measure because it is calculated with force and area. The units of pressure are Pascals (Pa), where the force is in Newtons (N) and area is in squared metres (m²).

$$\text{Pressure} = \frac{\text{Force}}{\text{Area}} \qquad \text{Area} = \frac{\text{Force}}{\text{Pressure}} \qquad \text{Force} = \text{Pressure} \times \text{Area}$$

Example:

A force of 63 N acts on a surface of 10m², calculate the pressure.

Step 1: Identify the correct formula (using the triangle: P = F ÷ A).
Step 2: Input the numbers being careful of units.
Pressure = 63 ÷ 10 = **6.3 N/m²** or **6.3 Pa.**

Practice questions:

Calculate the pressure on an object when:

Clearly state the units of your answer

a) A force of 20N is applied to a 4m² area

b) A force of 85N is applied to a 5m² area

c) A force of 98N is applied to a 16m² area

d) A force of 9N is applied to a 0.4m² area

e) A force of 27N is applied to a 540cm² area

Practice questions:

Calculate the force (N) placed on an object if :

Clearly state the units of your answer

f) An area of 16m² is under a pressure of 7 Pa

g) An area of 100m² is under a pressure of 14 Pa

h) An area of 55m² is under a pressure of 24 Pa

i) An area of 0.2m² is under a pressure of 12 Pa

j) An area of 500cm² is under a pressure of 2 Pa

Practice questions:

Calculate the area, in m², if :

Clearly state the units of your answer

k) A force of 18N is under 6 Pa of pressure

l) A force of 27N is under 10 Pa of pressure

m) A force of 100N is under 8 Pa of pressure

n) A force of 56N is under 14 Pa of pressure

o) A force of 1020N is under 4 Pa of pressure

Exam question:

A force of 84N is exerted by a cube which has a side length of 4m.
Calculate the pressure exerted by the cube.

(2)

Interpreting distance time graphs

Distance time graphs show you how far away something is from a starting point.
Distance goes on the y-axis and time goes on the x-axis.

Example: Interpret the distance time graph:

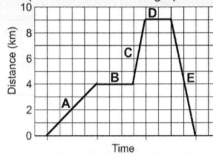

A: Moving away at a constant speed.
B: Graph is flat so stationary.
C: Moving away at a constant speed (faster than A).
D: Stationary.
E: Moving back towards the start at a constant speed.

Practice questions:

Interpret the distance time graphs by describing what is happening at each letter given:

a)
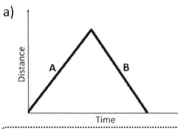

A

B

b)
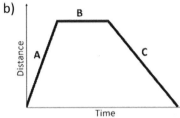

A

B

C

c)
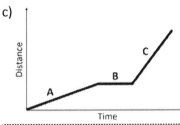

A

B

C

d)
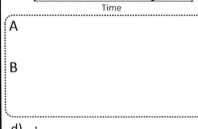

A

B

C

e)

A

f)

A

B

C

Exam question:

Here are 5 distance time graphs.
Each sentence in the table describes one of the graphs.
Write the letter of the correct graph next to each sentence.

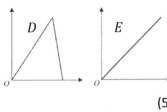

Travels away from home at a constant speed.	
Travels away from home and then returns home at a faster speed.	
Travels away from home stops for a while then continues away from home.	
Is away from home (stationary) and then returns home at a constant speed.	
Travels away from home, stops and then returns home.	

(5)

Distance time graphs - speed

You can calculate the speed from a distance time graph.
Speed = distance ÷ time, Average speed = total distance ÷ total time.   **Speed is the gradient of the line.**

Example:

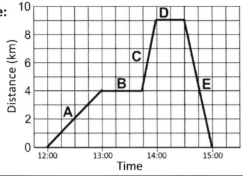

a) Find the speed of part A of the journey
Speed = distance ÷ time
= 4 ÷ 1 = **4 km/h**

b) Find the **average** speed of the journey
Total distance = 9 + 9 = 18km   *(height of the graph)*
Total time = 12pm to 3pm = 3 hrs

Average speed = 18 ÷ 3 = **6 km/h**

Practice questions:

Calculate the speed of **each** sloping part of the graphs:

a)
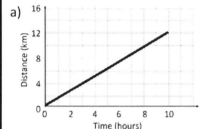

b)

c)
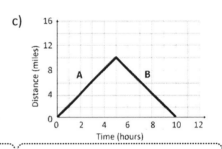

d)
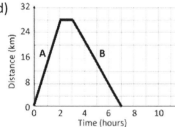

e)

f)
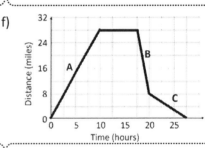

g) Calculate the *average* speed of **d)**   h) Calculate the *average* speed of **e)**   i) Calculate the *average* speed of **f)**

Exam question:

Brian drove 40 kilometres, from his home to Leeds.
He stopped and visited his friend Tom on the way.

a) Work out Brian's speed for the first part of his trip.
b) How long did Brian spend visiting Tom?
c) Calculate Brian's *average* speed for the "whole" journey.

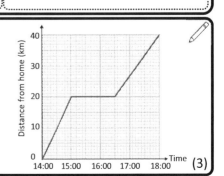

(3)

Interpreting velocity (speed) time graphs

Velocity time graphs show you how fast something is moving at a given time.
Velocity goes on the y-axis and time goes on the x-axis.

Example: Interpret the velocity time graph:

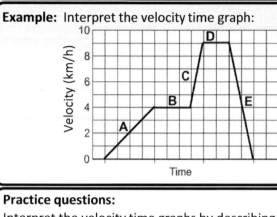

A: Constant acceleration.
B: Constant velocity.
C: Constant acceleration (faster than A).
D: Constant velocity.
E: Constant deceleration.

Practice questions:

Interpret the velocity time graphs by describing what is happening at each letter given:

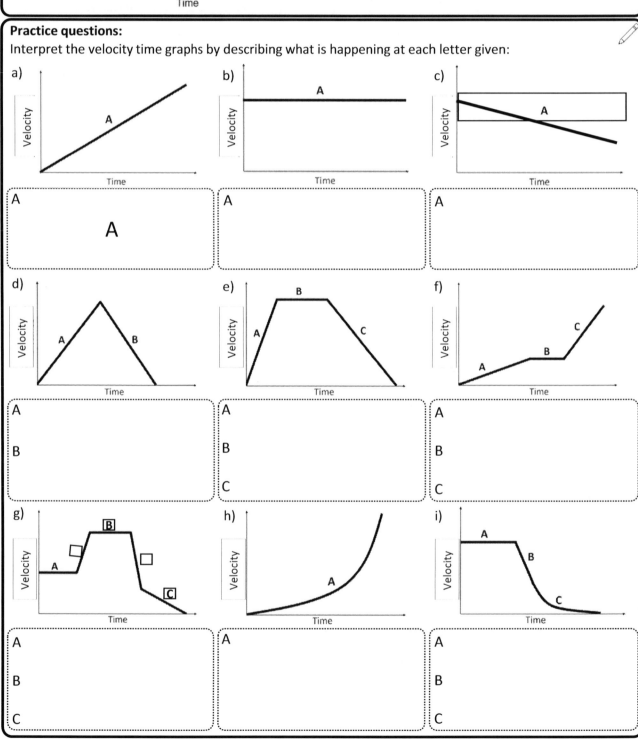

a)

A

A

b)

A

c)

A

d)

A

B

e)

A

B

C

f)

A

B

C

g)

A

B

C

h)

A

i)

A

B

C

Constructions – perpendicular bisector of a line

You need to be able to construct a perpendicular bisector using only a pair of compasses and a ruler. You must ensure that your 'construction' lines are clear.

Perpendicular bisector of a line instructions:

Step 1: Place the point of a compass on one end of the line and open it, so that it pencil end, beyond the halfway point of the line.

Step 2: Draw an arc above and below the line.

Step 3: Move the point of the compass to the other end of the line (keeping it the same size).

Step 4: Draw another arc above and below the line.

Step 5: Join the points where the arcs cross with a ruler to form the perpendicular bisector.

Note: This line goes through the midpoint at "right angles to (perpendicular) to the original line.

Practice questions:

Construct the perpendicular bisectors of the lines (using a pair of compasses):

a)

b)

c)

d)

Constructions – angle bisector

You need to be able to construct an angle bisector by using just a pair of compasses and a ruler. You must ensure that your 'construction' lines are clear.

Angle bisector instructions:

Step 1: Place the point of the compass at the corner of the two lines and open.

Step 2: Draw an arc through both of the lines that are creating the angle.

Step 3: Keeping the compass at the same width, place the point where the arc crosses the line and draw an arc in between the lines.

Step 4: Repeat the process from the other crossing point.

Step 5: Draw a line to the point where the two arcs cross to make the angle bisector.

Angle a = Angle b

Practice questions:

Construct an angle bisector for the angles shown (using a pair of compasses):

a)

b)

c)

d)

Scale drawings (maps)

A scale drawing is used to accurately show large things on a small scale. The amount something has been shrunk by is given as a ratio. 1:50 means the scale drawing is 50 times smaller than in real life.
Scales are used in maps to help you find distances in real life.

Example: Area of shapes

a) A waterfall is located 50m North of a tree.
   Mark the waterfall on the map

Distance on map = 50 ÷ 5000 = 0.01m = **1cm**

b) How far away is the cave from the tree?

Distance on map = 2cm   →   0.02m x 5000 = **200m**

Careful with units:
1m = 100cm
or 0.01m = 1cm

Waterfall
1cm   2cm   Cave
Tree
Scale 1:5000

Practice questions:

Using the map provided:

Volcano

Mine

Windmill

Cabin

Lagoon

SCALE 1:8000

Calculate the distance from:

a) The cabin to the mine

b) The lagoon to the windmill

c) The volcano to the cabin

d) The mine to the windmill

e) The cabin to the lagoon

f) The mine to the volcano

g) The lagoon to the volcano

h) The windmill to the volcano

Mark on the map the following locations:

i) The lighthouse which is located 200 metres north of the windmill.

j) The cave which is located 80 metres south of the lagoon.

k) The village which is located 440 metres west of the mine.

l) The ruins which are located 300 metres south east of the cabin.

Circumference of a circle

You need to use π to calculate the circumference of circles. There is a π button on scientific calculators, but π = 3.142 is often used when the π button is not available. To calculate the circumference you multiply π by the diameter. The formula is **Circumference = π x diameter**   (or c = 2πr since diameter = 2 x radius)

Examples:

Calculate the circumference of the circles.

 11cm

Circumference
= π x diameter
= π x 11 = **34.6 cm**

 7m

Diameter = 2 x radius = 2 x 7 = 14cm

Circumference
= π x diameter
= π x 14 = **44.0 cm**

Practice questions:

Calculate the circumference of these circles (leave your answer correct to 2 decimal places):

a) 5cm

b) 12cm

c) 3m

d) 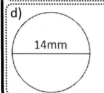 14mm

e) 24cm

f) 9.8mm

Practice questions:

Calculate the circumference of the these circles (leave your answer correct to 2 decimal places):

g) 4cm

h) 9cm

i) 17mm

j) 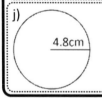 4.8cm

k) 13.7mm

l) 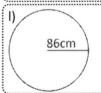 86cm

You may be asked for the "perimeter" of a semi-circle. You must work out ½ the full circumference of the whole circle, and then add on the diameter.

Examples

Calculate the perimeter of the semi-circle.

 6cm

Circumference = π x diameter = π x 6 = 18.8...cm
Arc = 18.85 ÷ 2 = 9.42
Perimeter = 9.42 + 6 = **15.42cm**

Practice questions:

Calculate the perimeter of the these semi-circles (to 2 decimal places):

m) 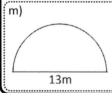 13m

n) 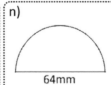 64mm

o) 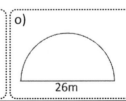 26m

Exam question:

The diameter of a bike's wheel 0.6m.
Calculate the circumference of the wheel.
Give your answer correct to 2 decimal places.

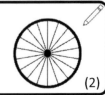

(2)

Area of a circle

You need to use π to calculate the area of circles. There is a π button on scientific calculators, but π = 3.142 is often used when the π button is not available. The formula is **Area = π x radius²** (A = πr²)

Examples:

Calculate the area of the circles.

Area
$= \pi \times r^2$
$= \pi \times 3^2$
$= \textbf{28.3 cm}^2$

Radius = diameter ÷ 2
$= 8 \div 2 = 4$cm
Area $= \pi \times 4^2$
$= \pi \times 16 = \textbf{50.3 cm}^2$

Practice questions:
Calculate the area of the these circles (leave your answer correct to 2 decimal places):

a)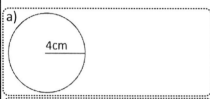
4cm

b)
9cm

c)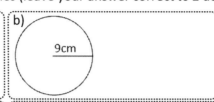
17mm

d)
4.8cm

e)
10.4m

f)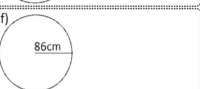
86cm

Practice questions:
Calculate the area of these circles (leave your answer correct to 2 decimal places):

g)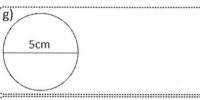
5cm

h)
12cm

i)
3m

j)
14mm

k)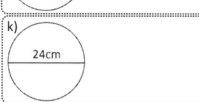
24cm

l)
9.8mm

You may be asked for the area of a circle 'in terms of π', this is for non-calculator papers.
You simply do the multiplication of the numbers and leave π tagged on the end.

Example:

Calculate the area of this circle in terms of π.

7cm

Area $= \pi \times r^2$
$= \pi \times 7^2 = \pi \times 49 = \textbf{49}\pi \textbf{ cm}^2$

Practice questions:
Calculate the area of the these circles in terms of π:

m)
5cm

n)
8cm

o)
12cm

Exam question:

The radius of a circle is 3.60 m.
Work out the area of the circle.
Give your answer correct to 3 significant figures.

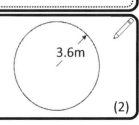
3.6m

(2)

Circle theorems – tangents and chords

A line from the centre of a circle (radius) forms a right angle with a tangent.	Two tangents are the same length from circle to where they meet. 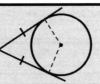	A radius bisects a chord at a right angle

Example:

Find the value of y

Step 1: Recognise that that you have two radius' which meets a tangent, therefore two 90° angles.

Step 2: Since angles in a quadrilateral sum to 360°

$y = 360 - (40 + 90 + 90) =$ **140°**

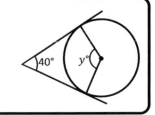

Practice questions: **Diagrams not drawn to scale**

Calculate the value of x in these diagrams:

a)
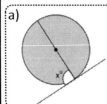

b)
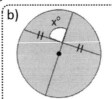

c)
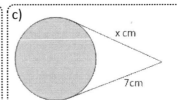

d)
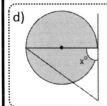

e)
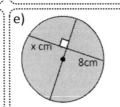

f)
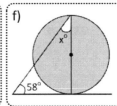

g)
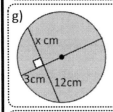

h)
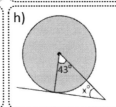

i)
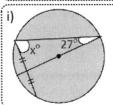

j)
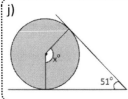

k)
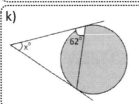

l)
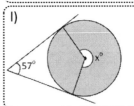

m)
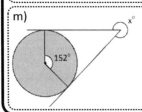

n)
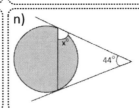

o)
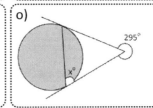

Exam question:

AB and AC are tangents to the circle.

O is the centre of the circle

Angle BAC = 50°

Calculate the size of angle BOC.

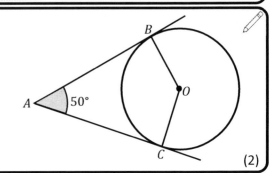

(2)

Pythagoras' theorem

Pythagoras' theorem only works in **right angled** triangles.
It is used to find a missing side when the other two sides are known.

Pythagoras' Theorem states that $a^2 + b^2 = c^2$ (where c must be the hypotenuse).

The **hypotenuse** is always opposite the right angle.

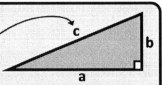

Examples:

a) Find the length of the hypotenuse.

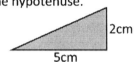

2cm

5cm

$a^2 + b^2 = c^2$
$2^2 + 5^2 = c^2$
$4 + 25 = c^2$
$29 = c^2$
$\sqrt{29} = c$
c = 5.39cm to 2d.p

b) Find the length of the hypotenuse.

7cm

9cm

$a^2 + b^2 = c^2$
$7^2 + 9^2 = c^2$
$49 + 81 = c^2$
$130 = c^2$
$\sqrt{130} = c$
c = 11.40cm to 2d.p

Practice questions:

Calculate the length of the missing side (hypotenuse) of the right angled triangles:

a)

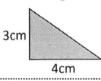

3cm

4cm

b)

12cm

35cm

c)

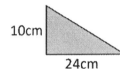

10cm

24cm

d)

12cm

5cm

e) To 2 decimal places

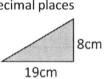

8cm

19cm

f) To 2 decimal places

43m

21m

g) To 2 decimal places

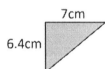

7cm

6.4cm

h) To 2 decimal places

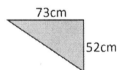

73cm

52cm

i) To 2 decimal places

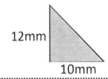

12mm

10mm

Exam question:

2 joggers start a run from the same spot.
The first travels south east and the other south west.
They both jog for 12 miles at the same speed.
How far apart are the two joggers?

Give your answer to 2 decimal places.

(2)

Pythagoras' theorem (2)

Pythagoras' theorem can also be use in right angled triangles to find the length of a smaller side. You must subtract the squared values instead of adding them.

Pythagoras' Theorem states that $a^2 + b^2 = c^2$ (where c must be the hypotenuse.)

As the **hypotenuse** is always the biggest you always start with this.

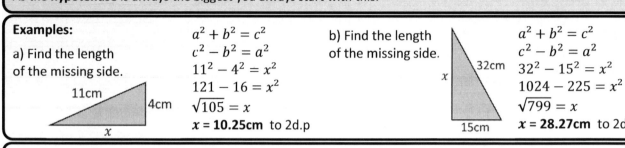

Examples:

a) Find the length of the missing side.

11cm · 4cm · x

$a^2 + b^2 = c^2$
$c^2 - b^2 = a^2$
$11^2 - 4^2 = x^2$
$121 - 16 = x^2$
$\sqrt{105} = x$
$x = 10.25\text{cm}$ to 2d.p

b) Find the length of the missing side.

32cm · x · 15cm

$a^2 + b^2 = c^2$
$c^2 - b^2 = a^2$
$32^2 - 15^2 = x^2$
$1024 - 225 = x^2$
$\sqrt{799} = x$
$x = 28.27\text{cm}$ to 2d.p

Practice questions:

Calculate the length of the missing side of these right angled triangles:

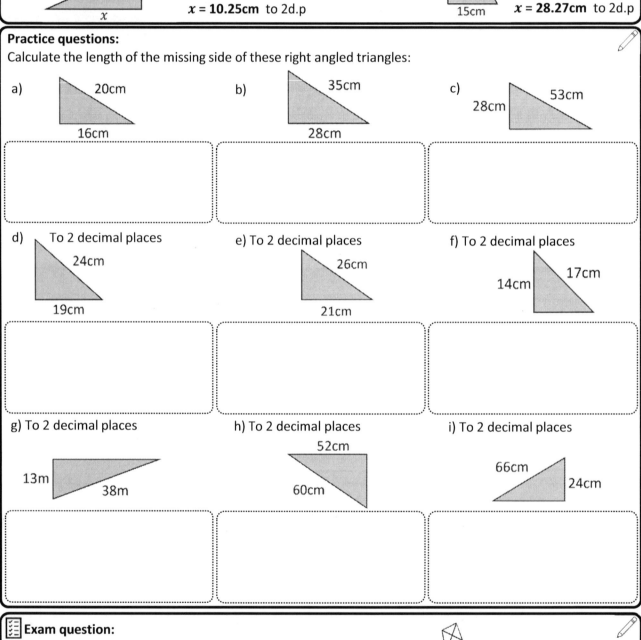

a) 20cm · 16cm

b) 35cm · 28cm

c) 28cm · 53cm

d) To 2 decimal places · 24cm · 19cm

e) To 2 decimal places · 26cm · 21cm

f) To 2 decimal places · 17cm · 14cm

g) To 2 decimal places · 13m · 38m

h) To 2 decimal places · 52cm · 60cm

i) To 2 decimal places · 66cm · 24cm

Exam question:

Shari went to a level field to fly a kite.

She let out all 650 feet of the string and tied it to a stake on the floor.

She walked out on the field until she was directly under the kite, which was 600 feet from the stake.

How high (h) was the kite from the ground?

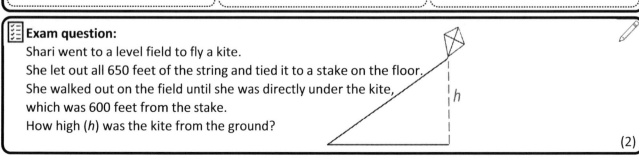

(2)

Introduction to trigonometry – sin, cos and tan

Trigonometry is used to calculate missing sides and angles **in right angled** triangles.
You need to be able to identify the names of the sides of a triangle to use trigonometry.

Hypotenuse – the longest side. Always opposite the right angle.

Adjacent – the side between right angle and the angle you are working with.

Opposite – the side opposite the angle you are working with.

Examples:

Identify the names of sides marked with a question mark.

Practice questions:

Identify the names of the sides marked with a question mark (?) (Hypotenuse, Adjacent or Opposite).

a)

b)

c)

d)

e)

f)

g)

h)

Sine, cosine & tangent are functions (often referred to as sin, cos & tan), which give you the ratio between two sides. You need to put the angle into the function to get the ratio.

$$\sin(x) = \frac{Opposite}{Hypotenuse} \qquad \cos(x) = \frac{Adjacent}{Hypotenuse} \qquad \tan(x) = \frac{Opposite}{Adjacent}$$

The ratios are usually abbreviated to form the following mnemonic: **SOH   CAH   TOA**

For GCSE – Your calculator must be working in degrees.
Make sure it says **Deg** or **D** at the top of your calculator.

Examples

Identify which trigonometric ratio is being used from the given sides of the triangles.

$\_\_\_\_(x) = \frac{18}{23}$

Sides used are O and H → **sin**

$\_\_\_\_(30°) = \frac{64}{x}$

Sides used are A and H → **cos**

Practice questions:

Identify the trigonometric ratio (sin, cos or tan) which are used in the triangles:

i) _____ $(x) = \frac{4}{8}$

j) _____ $(x) = \frac{5}{8}$

k) _____ $(x) = \frac{12}{19}$

l) _____ $(x) = \frac{3}{5}$

m) _____ $(x) = \frac{24}{31}$

n) _____ $(48°) = \frac{31}{x}$

o) _____ $(55°) = \frac{17}{x}$

p) _____ $(36°) = \frac{3}{x}$

93

Trigonometry – finding sides

When working out a missing side/angle of a right angled triangle, you must have a minimum of 2 pieces of information to use trigonometry.
To find a missing side, you must have one side and angle (other than the right angle).
The side you are given and the side you are trying to find, will dictate which ratio we use.

TIP: If you are given two sides, you can use Pythagoras to find the other side.

Examples:
Calculate the value of the missing side (marked b).

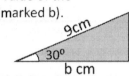

Step 1: Identify which function to use:
You have the hypotenuse and need the adjacent. $\cos(x) = \frac{Adjacent}{Hypotenuse}$

Step 2: Substitute in the values from the triangle. $\cos(30) = \frac{b}{9}$

Step 3: Re-arrange. $9 \times \cos(30) = b$

b = 7.79 to 2 d.p

Practice questions:
Calculate the length of the side **x** (Give your answer to 2 decimal places):

a)
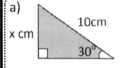

b)
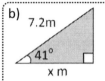

c)
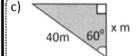

d)
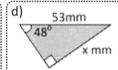

e)
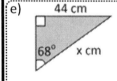

f)
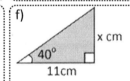

g)
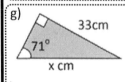

h)
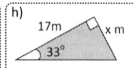

i)
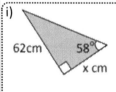

j)
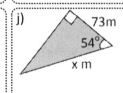

📋 **Exam question:**

The diagram shows a right angled triangle ABC.
Find the length of BC to 1 decimal place.

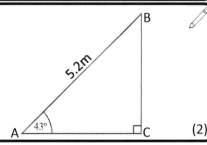

(2)

Trigonometry – finding angles

To find a missing angle, you must have two sides of a right angled triangle. The sides given will dictate which function you should use.

$$\sin(x) = \frac{Opposite}{Hypotenuse} \qquad \cos(x) = \frac{Adjacent}{Hypotenuse} \qquad \tan(x) = \frac{Opposite}{Adjacent}$$

You must use the **"inverse** function" on your calculator when calculating an angle.

Examples:
Calculate the value of the missing angle (marked x).

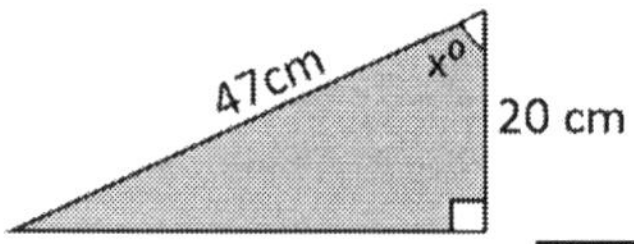

Step 1: Identify which function to use: You have the hypotenuse and adjacent. $\cos(x) = \frac{Adjacent}{Hypotenuse}$

Step 2: Substitute in the values from the triangle. $\cos(x) = \frac{20}{47}$

Step 3: Use the inverse function. $x = \cos^{-1}\left(\frac{20}{47}\right)$

47cm   x°   20 cm

⌨ *Using a calculator*   SHIFT COS 2 0 ÷ 4 7) $x = 64.8°$ **to 1 d.p**

Practice questions:
Calculate the angles marked **x** (Give your answer to 2 decimal places):

a)
8cm
11cm
x°

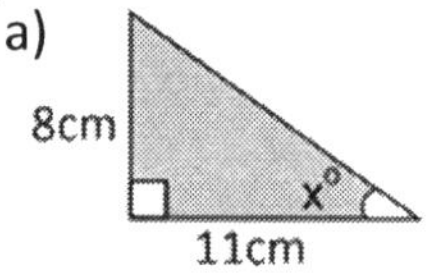

b)
25cm
20cm
x°

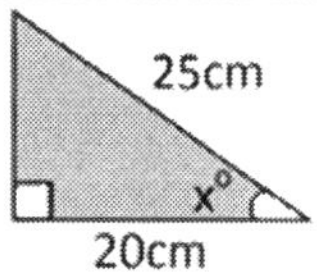

c)
16m
10m
x°

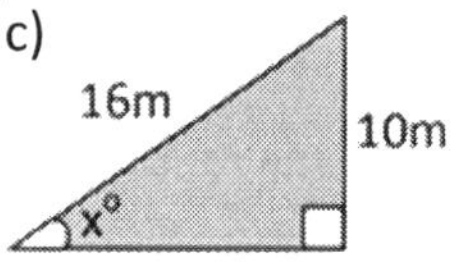

d)
14cm   x°   8cm

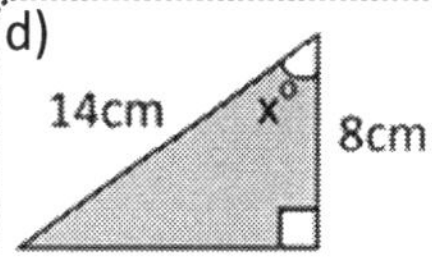

e)
63m
35m
x°

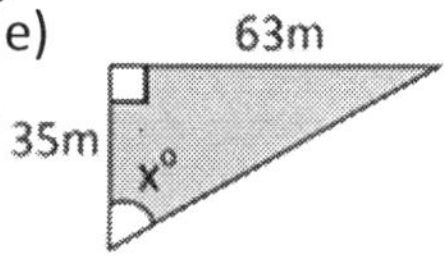

f)
55cm
66cm
x°

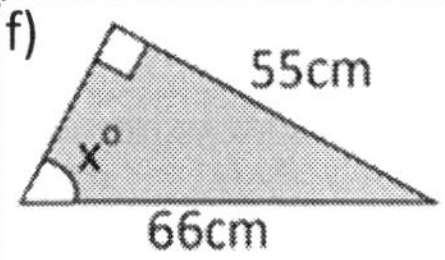

g)
26cm
30cm
x°

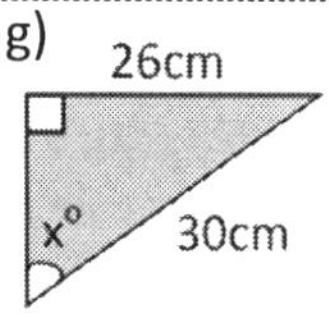

h)
36cm
42cm
x°

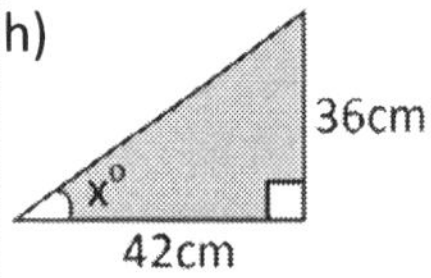

i)
70mm
58mm
x°

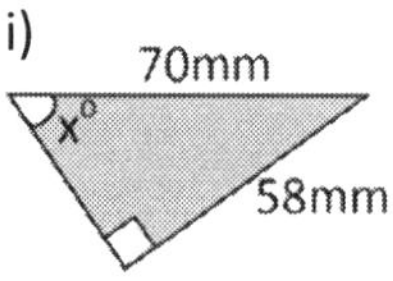

j)
8.6m   5.1m
x°

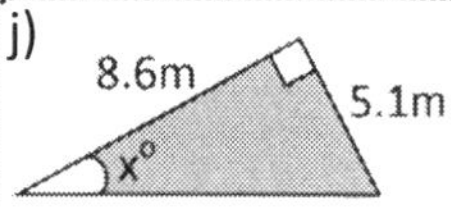

📋 **Exam question:**
The diagram shows a right angled triangle ABC.
AB = 6cm and AC = 13cm.
Find the size of angle BCA to 1 decimal place.

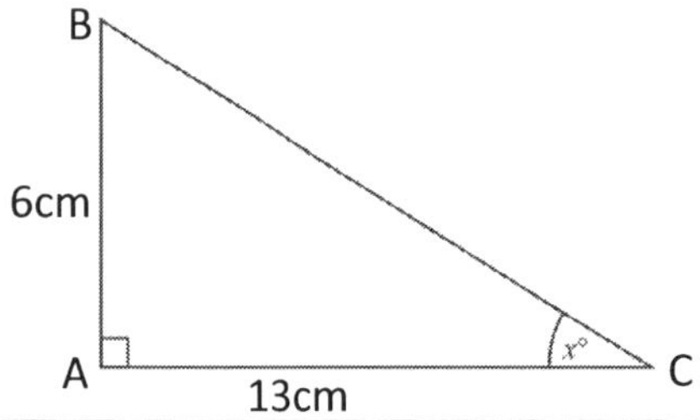

B
6cm
A   13cm   C   x°   (2)

95

Trigonometry – with bearings

You sometimes need to use trigonometry to find bearings.

Examples:
Tim walks 3km South then 7km East. Find the bearing of Tim's new position from his starting point.

Step 1: Draw a diagram

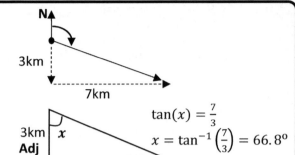

Step 2: Find the angle needed in the right angled triangle

Step 3: Use the found angle to find the bearing

66.8

$$\tan(x) = \frac{7}{3}$$

$$x = \tan^{-1}\left(\frac{7}{3}\right) = 66.8°$$

$$\mathbf{Bearing = 180 - 66.8 = 113.2°}$$

Practice questions:

Calculate the bearing of the final position from the starting position:

a) Sam walks 4km North then 5km East

b) Jim walks 8km South then 9km East

c) Pam walks 2km North then 6km West

d) Kim walks 5km South then 11km West

Converting units

Units are used to support with sizing of measurements, so it is important that you are aware of the metric conversions of lengths, mass and volume :

Length :
10mm = 1cm — To convert cm to mm, you must multiply by 10
100cm = 1m — To convert m to cm, you must multiply by 100
1000m = 1km — To convert km to m, you must multiply by 1000

Mass :
1000mg = 1g — To convert g to mg, you must multiply by 1000
1000g = 1kg — To convert kg to g, you must multiply by 1000
1000kg = 1T — To convert T to kg, you must multiply by 1000

Volume :
1000ml = 1L — To convert L to ml, you must multiply by 1000
100cl = 1L — To convert L to cl, you must multiply by 100
10ml = 1cl — To convert cl to ml, you must multiply by 10

If you are converting the other ways you must divide instead of multiplying.

Tip:
If you are converting to a smaller unit – you multiply.

If you are converting to a bigger unit – you divide.

Example:

Convert:
a) 7cm to mm
7 x 10 = **70mm**

b) 7mm to cm
7 ÷ 10 = **0.7cm**

c) 7kg to g
7 x 1000 = **7000g**

d) 7cl to L
7 ÷ 100 = **0.07L**

Practice questions:

Covert the following lengths:

a) 6m to cm

b) 9cm to mm

c) 5km to m

d) 4.1m to cm

e) 70mm to cm

f) 200cm to m

g) 2400m to km

h) 6cm to m

i) 24cm to mm

j) 70m to cm

k) 64mm to cm

l) 0.6km to cm

Covert the following masses:

a) 3kg to g

b) 8g to mg

c) 12T to kg

d) 7300kg to T

e) 4000mg to g

f) 900kg to T

g) 650g to kg

h) 67000g to T

i) 31T to g

j) 92T to kg

k) 720kg to mg

l) 0.63kg to mg

Covert the following volumes:

a) 9L to ml

b) 5cl to ml

c) 540cl to ml

d) 94L to cl

e) 800ml to cl

f) 3000ml to L

g) 9400ml to cl

h) 75000ml to L

i) 2200cl to L

j) 650cl to ml

k) 360ml to L

l) 2.54L to ml

Exam question:

A bucket weighs 600g.
When two thirds full with water, the bucket weighs 4kg.
Work out the total weight in kg when the bucket is fully filled with water.

(2)

Converting squared and cubed units

When converting squared units you must also square the conversion as you are working in two dimensions. e.g to convert cm to mm you multiply by 10, to change cm^2 to mm^2 you multiply by 10^2

Example:

Convert: a) $7m^2$ to cm^2

$7 \times 100^2 = \mathbf{70000cm^2}$

$\begin{array}{c} \mathbf{x\ 100} \\ m \longrightarrow cm \end{array}$

$\begin{array}{c} \mathbf{x\ 100^2} \\ m^2 \longrightarrow cm^2 \end{array}$

b) $7mm^2$ to cm^2

$7 \div 10^2 = \mathbf{0.07cm^2}$

$\begin{array}{c} \mathbf{\div\ 10} \\ mm \longrightarrow cm \end{array}$

$\begin{array}{c} \mathbf{\div\ 10^2} \\ mm^2 \longrightarrow cm^2 \end{array}$

Practice questions:

Covert the following units:

a) $11m^2$ to cm^2

b) $7cm^2$ to mm^2

c) $8km^2$ to m^2

d) $6m^2$ to cm^2

e) $90mm^2$ to cm^2

f) $60cm^2$ to m^2

g) $900m^2$ to km^2

h) $800cm^2$ to m^2

i) $50cm^2$ to mm^2

j) $420m^2$ to cm^2

k) $64mm^2$ to cm^2

l) $0.5km^2$ to cm^2

When converting cubed units you must also cube the conversion as you are working in three dimensions. e.g to convert cm to mm you multiply by 10, to change cm^3 to mm^3 you multiply by 10^3

Example:

Convert: a) $7m^3$ to cm^3

$7 \times 100^3 = \mathbf{7000000cm^3}$

$\begin{array}{c} \mathbf{x\ 100} \\ m \longrightarrow cm \end{array}$

$\begin{array}{c} \mathbf{x\ 100^3} \\ m^2 \longrightarrow cm^2 \end{array}$

b) $7mm^3$ to cm^3

$7 \div 10^3 = \mathbf{0.07cm^3}$

$\begin{array}{c} \mathbf{\div\ 10} \\ mm \longrightarrow cm \end{array}$

$\begin{array}{c} \mathbf{\div\ 10^3} \\ mm^3 \longrightarrow cm^3 \end{array}$

Practice questions:

Covert the following units:

m) $13m^3$ to cm^3

n) $7cm^3$ to mm^3

o) $8km^3$ to m^3

p) $5.6m^3$ to cm^3

q) $30mm^3$ to cm^3

r) $600cm^3$ to m^3

s) $5000m^3$ to km^3

t) $400cm^3$ to m^3

u) $70cm^3$ to mm^3

v) $500m^3$ to cm^3

w) $82mm^3$ to cm^3

x) $0.9km^3$ to cm^3

You need to be able to convert between cm^3 and litres.   **$1000cm^3 = 1$ litre**

Example:

Convert: a) $200cm^3$ to litres

$200 \div 1000 = \mathbf{0.2\ litres}$

b) 4 litres to cm^3

$4 \times 1000 = 4000\mathbf{cm^3}$

c) 4 litres to m^3

$4 \times 1000 = 4000cm^3$

$4000 \div 100^3 = \mathbf{0.004m^3}$

Practice questions:

Covert the following units:

y) $84cm^3$ to litres

z) 4 litres to cm^3

α) $600cm^3$ to litres

β) 50 litres to cm^3

γ) $900m^3$ to litres

δ) 4.7 litres to m^3

ε) $800mm^3$ to litres

μ) 60 litres to mm^3

Converting units of speed

When converting units of speed it is easiest to treat them like a ratio and take several steps to get to the desired units.

Example:

Convert: a) 7km/h to m/s

Answer: 1.944m/s

7km/h means 7km in 60 minutes

7km in 3600 seconds

7000m in 3600 seconds

1.944m in 1 seconds

(60 seconds in 1 minute)

(1km = 1000m)

(÷3600 to scale to 1 second)

Convert: a) 54m/s to km/h

Answer: 194.4km/h

54m/s means 54m in 1 second

3240m in 1 minute

194400m in 1 hour

194.4km in 1 hour

(x60 to get 1 minute)

(x60 to get 1 hour)

(1km = 1000m)

Practice questions:

Covert the following speeds:

a) 30km/h to m/s

b) 72km/h to m/s

c) 40m/s to km/h

d) 200km/h to m/s

e) 48m/s to km/h

f) 5.9m/s to km/h

g) 5.8km/h to m/s

h) 320m/s to km/h

i) 84.7km/h to m/s

99

Surface area of cubes and cuboids

The surface area of a 3D shape is sum of the area of all the faces. A **cube** has 6 faces which all have the same area. To find the surface area of a cube, you just need to work out the area of one face and multiply it by 6.

Example:

Find the surface area of the cube.

Don't forget units!

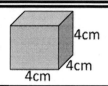

Area of face = base x height
= 4 x 4 = 16 cm²

Total Surface Area = 6 x 16 = **96 cm²**

Practice questions:

Calculate the surface of the cubes. State the units of your answer.

a)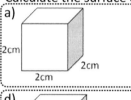

b)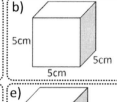

c)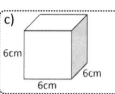

d)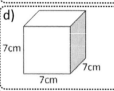

e)

f)

A **cuboid** has 6 faces. The opposite faces have the same area. To find the surface area of a cuboid, you need to work out the area of 6 faces then add them all together.

Example:

Find the surface area of the cuboid.

Don't forget units!

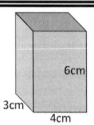

Area of front face = base x height = 4 x 6 = 24cm²
Area of side face = 3 x 6 = 18cm²
Area of top face = 3 x 4 = 12cm²

Because the opposite faces of the cuboid have the same area – we can use the same area twice.

Total Surface Area = 24 + 24 + 18 + 18 + 12 + 12 = 108cm²

Practice questions:

Calculate the surface of the cuboids:

g)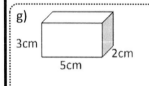

h)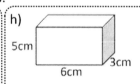

i)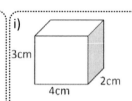

j)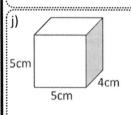

k)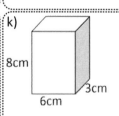

l)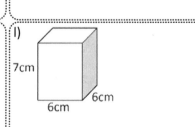

📋 **Exam question:**

A cuboid is drawn on a centimetre 3D coordinate grid, as shown.
Work out the surface area of cuboid.

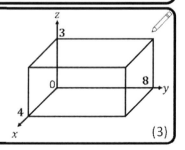

(3)

Volume of cubes and cuboids

Volume is the amount of space a 3D shape takes up. Volume has cubed units e.g: cm³, mm³, m³...
You can calculate volume of a shape by counting the number of cubes it is made up of.

Examples:

The following shapes are made up of cm cubes. Calculate the volume of each shape.

Volume = 5 cm³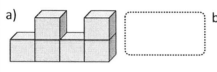

Volume = 4 cm³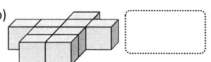

Volume = 7 cm³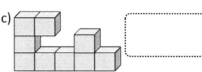

Practice questions:

Calculate the total volume of these shapes built from 1cm cubes:

a)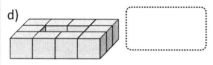

b)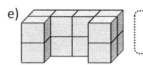

c)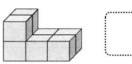

d)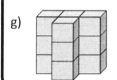

e)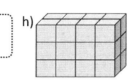

f)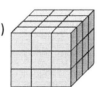

g)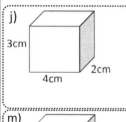

h)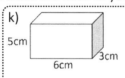

i)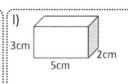

To calculate the volume of a cube or cuboid, you simply multiply the 3 dimensions together.

Example:

Find the volume of the cuboid.

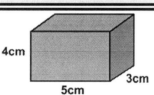

4cm, 5cm, 3cm

Volume = width x height x depth
= 4 x 5 x 3
= 60 cm³   **Don't forget units!**

Practice questions:

Calculate the volume of the cuboids. State the units of your answer.

j)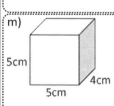
3cm, 2cm, 4cm

k)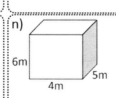
5cm, 3cm, 6cm

l)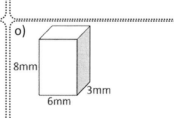
3cm, 2cm, 5cm

m)
5cm, 4cm, 5cm

n)
6m, 5m, 4m

o)
8mm, 3mm, 6mm

Exam question:

A cuboid is drawn on a centimetre 3D coordinate grid, as shown.
Work out the volume of the cuboid.

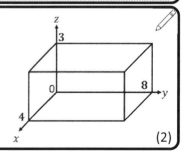

(2)

101

Volume of prisms and cylinders

A prism is a 3D shape which has the same cross-sectional area all the way through it.
The cross-sectional area is the area of the front and back face of the shape.
Volume of a prism = cross sectional area x length

Example:

Find the volume of the prism
State the units of your answer.

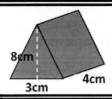

Step 1 : Work out the cross-sectional area (CSA)
Area of triangle = ½ x 8 x 3 = 12cm²
Step 2 : Multiply the CSA by the length
Volume = CSA x length = 12 x 4 = **48cm³**

Practice questions:
Calculate the volume of the prisms.

a)
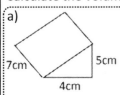

b)
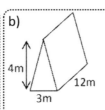

c)
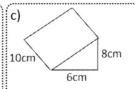

d)
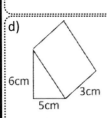

e)
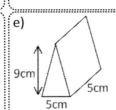

f)
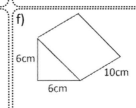

The cylinder is a prism whose cross-sectional area is a circle. The area of a circle is πr².
Volume of a cylinder = πr² x length

Examples

Find the volume of this cylinder.
State the units of your answer.

Step 1 : Work out the cross-sectional area (CSA).
Area of circle = π x r² = π x 3² = 28.27...cm²
Step 2 : Multiply the CSA by the length
Volume = CSA x length = 28.27... x 11 = **311cm³**

Practice questions:
Calculate the volume of the cylinders (give your answer correct to 3 significant figures):

g)
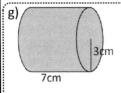

h)
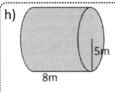

i)
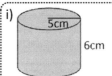

j)
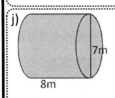

k)
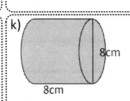

l)
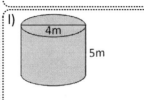

Exam question:

A wooden door stop is made of wood as
shown. The cost of wood is 0.1p per cm³.
What is the cost price the wooden door stop?

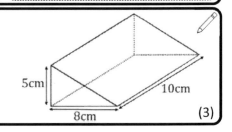

(3)

Surface area of a prism

The surface area of a prism is made up of two identical shapes and usually several rectangles. A triangular prism is made up of two triangles and three rectangles. The triangular faces are the same, but the rectangles could be different and you **may need to use Pythagoras' Theorem** to find missing dimensions.

Example:

Find the surface area of the prism.
State the units of your answer.

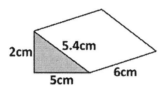

Step 1 : Work out the area of each face.
Area of base = 5 x 6 = 30cm²
Area of slope = 5.4 x 6 = 32.4cm²
Area of left face = 2 x 6 = 12cm²
Area of triangles = ½ x 5 x 2 = 5cm²
Total Surface Area = 30 + 32.4 + 12 + 5 + 5 = **84.4cm²**

Practice questions:
Calculate the surface area of the prisms:

a)
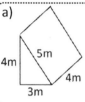

b)
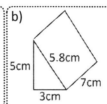

c)
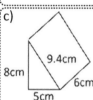

d)
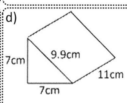

Examples

Find the surface area of the prism.
State the units of your answer.

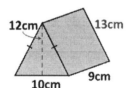

Step 1 : Find the length of the slope.
Slope = $\sqrt{5^2 + 12^2}$ = 13cm
Step 2 : Work out the area of the faces.
Area of base = 9 x 10 = 90cm²
Area of side faces = 9 x 13 = 117cm²
Area of triangles = ½ x 10 x 12 = 60cm²
Total Surface Area = 90 + 60 + 60 + 117 + 117 = **444cm²**

Practice questions:
Calculate the surface area of the prism:

e)
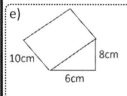

f)
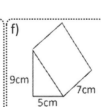

g)
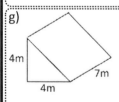

h)
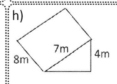

Exam question:

A door stop is to be gold plated.
Gold plating costs £2 per cm².
Calculate the cost of gold plating the door stop.

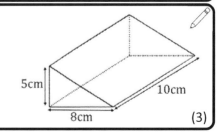

(3)

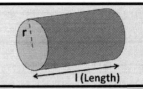

The surface area of a cylinder is made up of two circles and a rectangle.
The width of the rectangle is the circumference of the circle.

Surface area of a cylinder = 2πr² + 2πrl

l (Length)

Example:

Find the surface area
of the cylinder.
State the units of
your answer.

5cm

9cm

Step 1 : Work out the area of the circle.
Area of circle = π x r² = π x 5² = 78.5398cm²
Step 2 : Work out the area of the rectangle.
Area of rectangle = 2 x π x 5 x 9 = 282.7433cm²
Total Surface Area = 2(78.5398) + 282.74 = **439.82cm²**

Practice questions:

Calculate the surface area of the cylinders (leave your answer correct to 1 decimal place):

a)
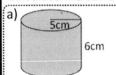
5cm
6cm

b)
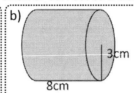
3cm
8cm

c)
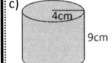
4cm
9cm

d)
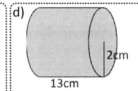
2cm
13cm

e)
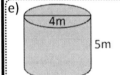
4m
5m

f)
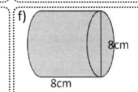
8cm
8cm

g)
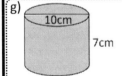
10cm
7cm

h)
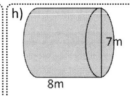
7m
8m

i)
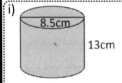
8.5cm
13cm

j)
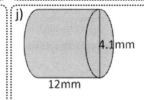
4.1mm
12mm

Exam question:

A cylinder has radius 5cm and height 4cm.
Write down an *expression* for the **surface area**
of the cylinder in terms of π.
Give your answer in its simplest form.

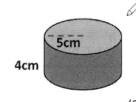
5cm
4cm

(3)

Similar shapes

Similar shapes are the same shape but different sizes. The **angles** in similar shapes are always the same.

2cm ■ ➡ 4cm ■
5cm
10cm

These shapes are 'similar' as both of the dimensions (lengths and widths) have been multiplied by the same scale factor of 2.

Example:
Calculate the missing side (?) in the similar shapes.

4cm SF = 3 ?
2cm 6cm

Step 1: Identify scale factor by dividing corresponding sides → 6 ÷ 2 = 3

Step 2: Multiply the other side by the scale factor to find the missing side → 4 x 3 = **12 cm**

Practice questions:
Calculate the value of x in the similar shapes:

a)
6cm 4cm

12cm x

b)
10cm
70°

20cm
x

c)
3cm 7cm

9cm x

d)
8cm
x

72cm
54cm

e)
7cm x

49cm
44°

f)
x
4cm

78cm
52cm

g)
14cm 10cm

x 15cm

h)
5cm 8cm

12cm x

i)
12cm
x

27cm
36cm

Exam question:

The diagram shows an hour-glass made from two similar pentagons.

Calculate the value of *h*.

2cm
2.5cm

h

3cm

(2)

105

Translations

A translation is when you move or slide a shape without changing it in any other way.

The picture shows the translation of shape A of 2 right and 4 down, to shape B.

You can check your answer by counting from any corner of the shape to the **same** corner of the translated shape.

Vectors are used to describe translations.

The <u>top</u> number tells you how far to move <u>left or right.</u>
The <u>bottom</u> number tells you how far to <u>up or down.</u>

In this example – shape A would have translated by the vector: $\begin{pmatrix} 2 \\ -4 \end{pmatrix}$

A positive number corresponds to right/up and a negative left/down.

Example:
Translate Shape A by the vector $\begin{pmatrix} 3 \\ -2 \end{pmatrix}$

Step 1: Identify the movement.
This means 3 right and 2 dow**n**.
Step 2: Select a vertex of the shape and count from that point.
Step 3: Draw the shape exactly the same in the new position.

Practice questions:
Translate the following shapes:

a) Right 3
   Down 3

b) Left 1
   Up 4

c) Left 1
   Down 3

d) i) $\begin{pmatrix} 3 \\ 4 \end{pmatrix}$ ii) $\begin{pmatrix} 0 \\ 2 \end{pmatrix}$

e) i) $\begin{pmatrix} 1 \\ 2 \end{pmatrix}$ ii) $\begin{pmatrix} -2 \\ 1 \end{pmatrix}$

f) i) $\begin{pmatrix} -1 \\ -2 \end{pmatrix}$ ii) $\begin{pmatrix} 3 \\ -1 \end{pmatrix}$

g) i) $\begin{pmatrix} -1 \\ 1 \end{pmatrix}$ ii) $\begin{pmatrix} 2 \\ 0 \end{pmatrix}$

h) i) $\begin{pmatrix} 2 \\ -1 \end{pmatrix}$ ii) $\begin{pmatrix} 1 \\ 3 \end{pmatrix}$

i) i) $\begin{pmatrix} 0 \\ 4 \end{pmatrix}$ ii) $\begin{pmatrix} 3 \\ 0 \end{pmatrix}$

Exam question:
Translate shape A by the vector $\begin{pmatrix} 6 \\ -5 \end{pmatrix}$

Label the shape with the letter B.

(2)

106

Describing translations

If a shape has been translated, you must state it has been translated and also give the vector that shows how far left/right and up/down the shape has been translated.

Example:

Describe the transformation that maps shape A onto shape B.

Step 1: Select a vertex of the shape and count from that point.

Step 2: Count the number of squares left/right it moves: **2 right**.

Step 3: Count the number of squares up/down it moves: **4 up**.

Step 4: Write as a vector (and state translated by).

Translated by the vector $\begin{pmatrix} 2 \\ 4 \end{pmatrix}$

Practice questions:

Describe the transformations of shape:

a) A to B

b) A to B

c) A to B

d) A to B

e) A to B

f) B to A

g) B to A

h) B to A

i) A to B

Reflections

A reflection is when you create a mirror image across a given line.
The image should be the same distance away from the line.

Example:

Reflect shape A in the mirror line given.

Step 1: Trace the shape **and** the mirror line.
Step 2: Flip the paper over on the mirror line.
Step 3: Copy the shape.

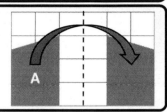

Practice questions:

Reflect the shape in the given mirror line:

a)
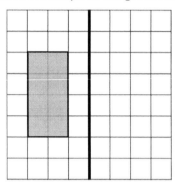

b)
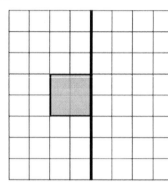

c)
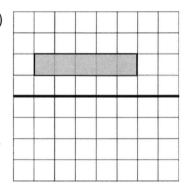

d)
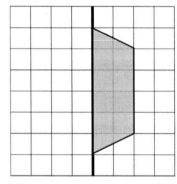

e)
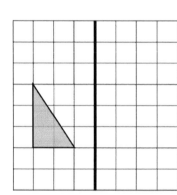

f)
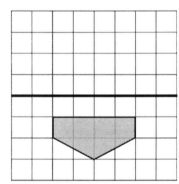

g)
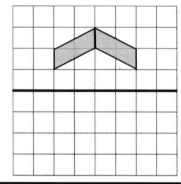

h)
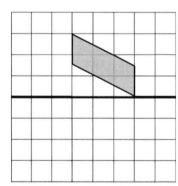

i)
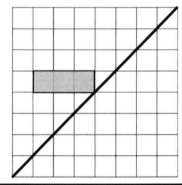

Exam question:

The point A with co-ordinate (3 , 3) is reflected in the mirror line shown ($y = 2$) to get point B.

State the co-ordinates of B.

Use can the grid to help you.

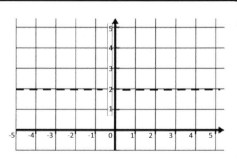

(1)

108

Equations of mirror lines

Sometimes you need to draw a reflection or describe a reflection with the "equation" of a mirror line.
Vertical mirror lines always take the form $x = ?$ Horizontal mirror lines always take the form $y = ?$

Example:
Reflect shape A in the line $x = 3$

Step 1: Find the value of 3 on the x axis and draw a vertical line.
Step 2: Trace the shape **and** the mirror line.
Step 3: Flip the paper over on the mirror line.
Step 4: Copy the shape.

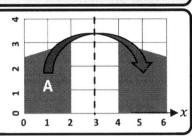

Practice questions:
Reflect the shape in the line:

a) $x = 3$

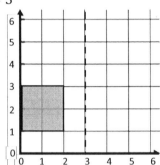

b) $y = 2$

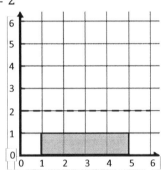

c) $y = 3$

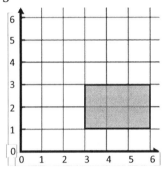

d) $y = 3$

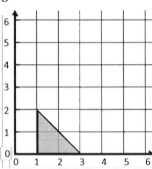

e) $x = 3$

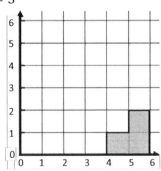

f) $x = 3$

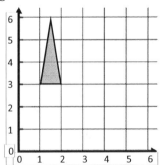

g) $x = -1$

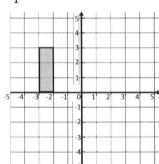

h) $y = 0$

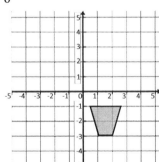

i) $x = 0$

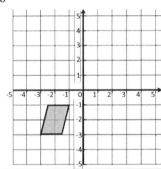

Exam question:

Shape A is reflected in the mirror line $y = 1$ to shape B.
Draw shape B.
Shape B is reflect in the mirror line $x = 1$ to shape C.
Draw shape C.

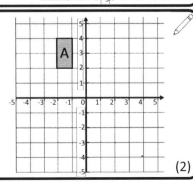

(2)

109

To describe a reflection, you must state the shape has been reflected, and also give the equation of the line it has been reflected in (referred to as a mirror line).

Example:

Describe the transformation of the shape A to shape B.

Step 1: Find the equation of the mirror line: $y = 3$

Step 2: State that it has been reflected and the equation of the mirror line.

Shape A has been reflected in the line $y = 3$

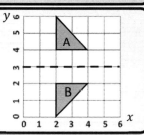

Practice questions:

Describe the transformation of shape:

a)
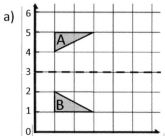

A to B

b)
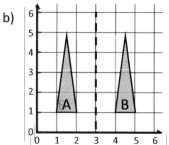

A to B

c)
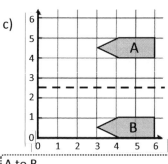

A to B

d)
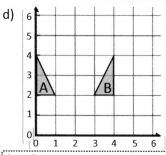

A to B

e)
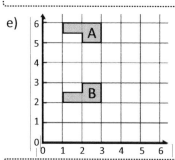

A to B

f)
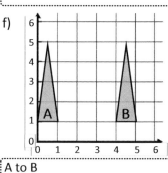

A to B

g)
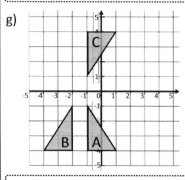

A to B

A to C

h)
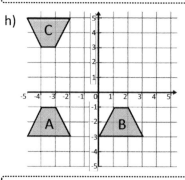

A to B

A to C

i)
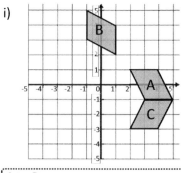

A to B

A to C

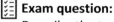

Exam question:

Describe the transformations that maps
shape A to shape B in the diagram shown.

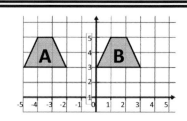

(2)

Rotations

Rotating a shape means you are turning it around a point.
The point of rotation is usually given as a co-ordinate.
You can rotate a shape clockwise or anti-clockwise.
The amount you rotate is given in degrees : 90° means a quarter turn, 180° means a half turn, 270° means a 3 quarters turn.

 anti-clockwise clockwise

Example:

Rotate shape A 90° clockwise about the marked point.

Step 1: Place tracing paper over grid.
Step 2: Copy the shape (A) onto the tracing paper.
Step 3: Place your pencil on the marked point.
Step 4: Rotate the shape 90° clockwise.
Step 5: Copy the shape onto the grid shown by the tracing paper.

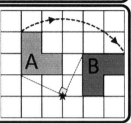

Practice questions:

Rotate the following shapes by the given angle and direction:

a) 180°

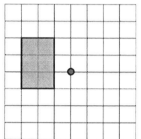

b) 90° clockwise

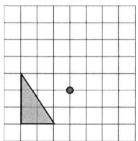

c) 90° anti-clockwise

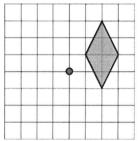

d) Rotate shape A 90° anti-clockwise about (3,3)

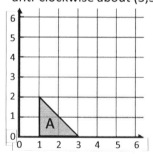

e) Rotate shape B 90° anti-clockwise about (3,0)

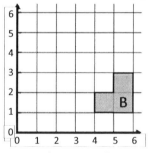

f) Rotate shape C 90° clockwise about (2,3)

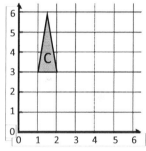

g) Rotate shape A 90° clockwise about (-1,0)

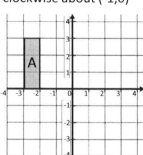

h) Rotate shape B 90° clockwise about (0,0)

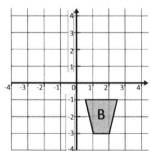

i) Rotate shape C 90° anti-clockwise about (-1,1)

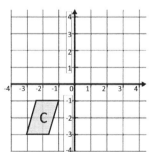

Exam question:

Rotate shape A 90° anti-clockwise around the point (0,-1).
Label this shape B.

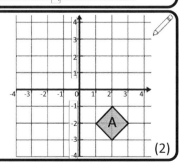

(2)

111

Describing Rotations

When describing a rotation of a shape you must state the following things:
1) That is has been rotated.
2) The direction and the angle it has been rotated.
3) The point it has been rotated about.

You can find the centre of rotation by using tracing paper and seeing where you need to place your pencil to get from shape A to shape B.

Example:

Describe the transformation from shape A to shape B.

Step 1: Identify the direction (clockwise).
Step 2: Determine the angle 90°.
Step 3: Find the centre of rotation by testing different co-ordinates (1,2).

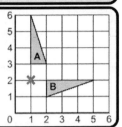

Answer: Shape A has been rotated 90° clockwise about the point (1,2)

Practice questions:

In each of the diagrams, describe the transformation of shape A to shape B:

a)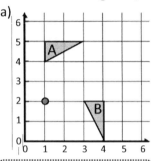

b)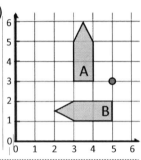

c)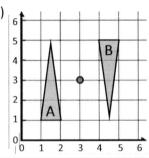

d)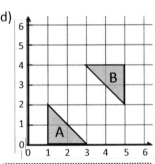

e)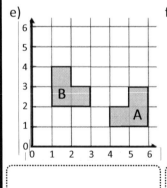

f)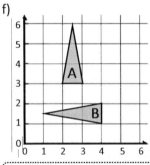

g)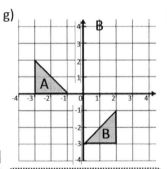

h)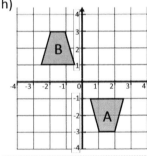

Exam question:

Fully describe the single transformation that maps shape **Q** onto shape **P**.

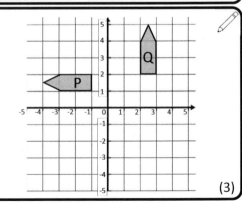

(3)

Enlargements – Scale Factors

An enlargement is when you change the size of a shape. The scale factor tells you how many times bigger the shape is. If a shape is 'enlarged' by a scale factor less then 1 – the shape will be smaller.

5cm
2cm
The lengths of the sides have doubled so scale factor = 2
10cm
4cm

Scale Factor = 3
4cm
2cm
12cm
6cm

Scale Factor = 1/5
10cm
5cm
2cm
1cm

Example:

Find the scale factors of these enlargements that transforms A to B:

a)
A
2cm
B
5cm

Step 1: Identify sides (5cm and 2cm)
Step 2: Divide 'enlarged' shape value by original value. $5 \div 2 = 2.5$
Scale Factor = 2.5

b)
A
10cm
B
4cm

Scale Factor $= 4 \div 10 = \dfrac{4}{10} = \dfrac{2}{5}$

Practice questions:

Find the scale factors of the enlargements:

a) 3cm
5cm
6cm
10cm

e) 9cm
72cm

b) 4cm 4cm
4cm
20cm 20cm
20cm

f) 24cm
22cm
12cm
11cm

c) 6cm
7cm
24cm
28cm

g) 48cm
36cm
12cm
9cm

d) 12cm
7cm
84cm
49cm

h) 6cm
9cm

Exam question:

Shape A has been 'enlarged' to form shape B.
Calculate the value of x.

30cm
24cm A
20cm
x cm B

(2)

Enlargements from a point

When a shape is enlarged from a point (*centre of enlargement*), not only is the shape enlarged by the given scale factor, but so is the distance from the centre of enlargement is also enlarged.

Example:

Enlarge the shape by a scale factor of 2 from the point (1,1):

Step 1: Pick a point on the shape and see how far away it is from the centre of enlargement (1,1).

Step 2: Multiply the distance of both horizontal and vertical by the scale factor, and mark the new point.

Step 3: Repeat for all corners of the shape.

HINT: If you draw lines from the centre of enlargement to each corresponding vertex (corner) – it will form a straight line as shown in the diagram.

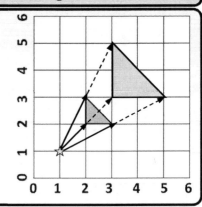

Practice questions:

For questions a, b and c, enlarge the shape by the given scale factors (anywhere on the grid):

a) Scale Factor 3

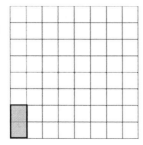

b) Scale Factor 2

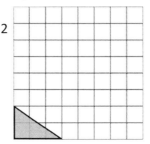

c) Scale Factor 2

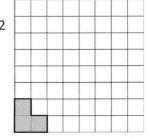

c) Enlarge the shape by a scale factor of 2 from the point (0,1)

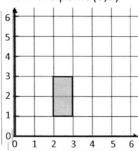

d) Enlarge the shape by a scale factor of 3 from the point (0,0)

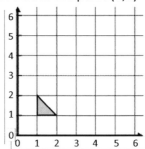

e) Enlarge the shape by a scale factor of 2 from the point (1,6)

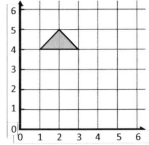

f) Enlarge the shape by a scale factor of 3 from the point (-3,-2)

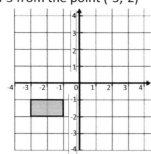

g) Enlarge the shape by a scale factor of 0.5 from the point (-1,3)

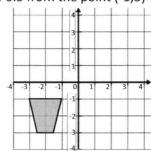

h) Enlarge the shape by a scale factor of 2 from the point (-1,-1)

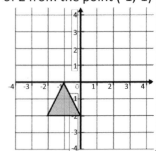

Exam question:

Enlarge the shape shown in the diagram by a scale factor of ½ from the point (-2,-3).

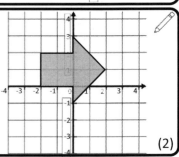

(2)

Finding centre of enlargements/describing enlargements

You can find the centre of enlargement by joining up the corresponding corners of the shapes.
The point where the lines intersect is the centre of enlargement

Example:
Find the centre of enlargement from shape A to shape B

Step 1: Draw lines from a vertex of the enlarged shape to the corresponding vertex of the original shape (but continue the line).
Step 2: Repeat for every vertex of the shape.
Step 3: Identify the co-ordinate where the lines meet – this is the centre of enlargement.

Centre of enlargement is at (0,1)

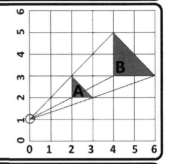

Practice questions:

Find the co-ordinates of the **centre of enlargement**:

a)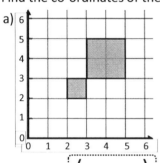

(,   )

b)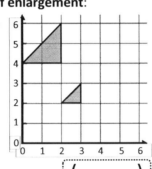

(,   )

c)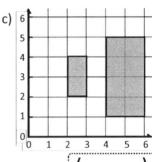

(,   )

d)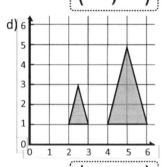

(,   )

e)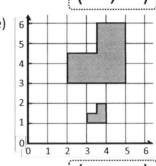

(,   )

f)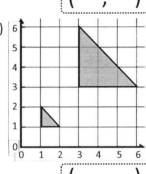

(,   )

g)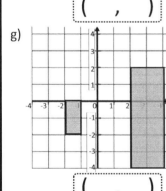

(,   )

h)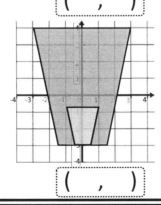

(,   )

i)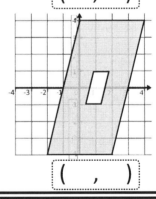

(,   )

Exam question:

Shape A has been enlarged to Shape B.
Find the centre of enlargement.

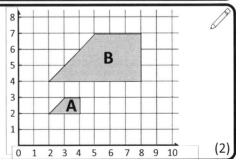

(2)

115

Mean calculations

Sometimes you are already given the mean and you need to find out missing pieces of information which are not given. You can multiply the mean by the number of values to get the total score.

Example:

10 students get their scores back after a test, 9 of the students have a mean of 40 on the test.
The average of all 10 students was 41. What score did the 10th student get?

Step 1: Calculate the total score of the **10** students.	41 x 10 = 410
Step 2: Calculate the total score of the **9** students.	40 x 9 = 360
Step 3: Find the difference to work out the 10th students score.	410 − 360 = 50
	The 10th person scored 50

Practice questions:

a) 4 students get a mean mark of 8 in a test.
   How many marks did they get altogether?

b) 8 students get a mean mark of 20 in a test.
   How many marks did they get altogether?

c) 5 students get a mean mark of 14 in a test.
   How many marks did they get altogether?

d) 6 students scored 48 marks in total.
   The mean mark of 5 of the students was 9.
   How many marks did the last student get?

e) 10 students scored 153 marks in total.
   The mean mark of 9 of the students was 15.
   How many marks did the last student get?

f) 12 students scored 261 marks in total.
   The mean mark of 11 of the students was 22.
   How many marks did the last student get?

g) 3 students got a mean of 11 marks in test. A
   4th students mark changed the mean to 12.
   How many marks did the 4th student get?

h) 8 students got a mean of 19 marks in test. A
   9th students mark changed the mean to 18.
   How many marks did the 9th student get?

i) 15 students got a mean of 13 marks in test. A
   16th students mark changed the mean to 13.5.
   How many marks did the 16th student get?

Exam question:

A product received 9 reviews with a mean score of 4.5 stars.
A 10th review was given which changed the star rating to 4.3.
What star rating did the 10th person give the product?

(2)

Combining mean calculations

Sometimes you are already given two mean averages of different group sizes and you need to combine them.

Example:

10 men have an average height of 1.75m and 20 women have an average height of 1.65m, what is the overall mean height?

Step 1: Calculate the total of the men's heights.	1.75 x 10 = 17.5
Step 2: Calculate the total of the women's heights.	1.65 x 20 = 33.0
Step 3: Find the total of all their heights.	33.0 + 17.5 = 50.5
Step 4: Find the overall mean by dividing the total by 30 (10 + 20).	505 ÷ 30 = 1.683
	The overall average is 1.683m

Practice questions:

5 boys have a mean score of 9 and 3 girls gave a mean score of 11 on a test.

a) i) What is the total score of the boys?

ii) What is the total score of girls?

iii) What is the total score of everyone?

iv) What is the overall mean score?

b) 8 boys have a mean score of 12 and 7 girls gave a mean score of 11 on a test.

Calculate the overall mean score on the test.

c) 15 men have a mean height of 1.65m and 12 women have a mean height of 1.6m.

Calculate the overall mean height.

d) 7 dogs have a mean weight of 7.6kg and 11 cats have a mean weight of 4.5kg.

Calculate the overall mean weight.

Exam question:

30 runners complete a marathon. 18 were under 30 years old, and the rest 30 or over.
The mean time for under 30s was 3 hours 15 minutes, and the mean time for everyone 30 or over was 4 and half hours.
What was the mean time for all 30 runners?

(3)

Combining mean calculations (2)

Sometimes you are already given the overall mean of two groups and need to find the mean of one group.

Example:

8 men and 12 women have an overall average height of 1.72m.

The men have an average height of 1.85m. what is the mean height of the women?

Step 1: Calculate the total of the men's heights.	1.85 x 8 = 14.8
Step 2: Calculate the total of the everyone's height. (8 + 12 = 20)	1.72 x 20 = 34.4
Step 3: Find the total of all the women's heights.	34.4 - 14.8 = 19.6
Step 4: Find the women's mean by dividing the total by 12.	19.6 ÷ 12 = 1.633
	The women's average is 1.633m

Practice questions:

30 boys and 40 girls have a mean score of 16 on a test. The boys' mean is 14.6.

a) i) What is the total score of the boys?

  ii) What is the total score of everyone?

  iii) What is the total score of the girls?

  iv) What is the mean score of the girls?

b) 5 boys and 8 girls have an overall mean score of 32 on a test. The girls mean is 29.

Calculate the mean score of the boys.

c) 24 men and 28 women have an overall mean height of 1.66m. The women have a mean height of 1.55m.

Calculate the mean height of the men.

d) 42 dogs and 36 cats have a total mean weight of 6.3kg. The dogs have a mean weight of 8.2kg.

Calculate the mean weight of the cats.

Exam question:

50 runners complete a marathon. 20 were under 30 years old, and the rest were 30 or over.

The overall mean time was 3 hours 15 minutes, and the mean time for everyone 30 or over was 3 hours 45 minutes.

What was the mean time for the runners under 30 years old?

(3)

Mode and median from a frequency table

Mode: The mode is the value which occurs most, which is the value in the table with the highest frequency.

Example:

Identify the mode number of siblings from the table of results shown:

The highest frequency in the frequency column is 22, this means that the mode is 2 as most people have 2 siblings. → **Mode = 2**

Please note: The answer is **NOT** 22. This is just the frequency of people with 2 siblings.

No. of Siblings	Frequency
0	6
1	11
2	22
3	8
4	2

Median: The median is the middle value when results are listed in order.
You can find where the middle value lies by adding 1 to the total and dividing by 2.

Example

Identify the median number of siblings from the table shown:

Median position is (50 + 1) ÷ 2 = 25.5.
So the median value is the 25.5th value.
Add up the frequencies until you get to the 25.5th value.
The 25.5th value lies in the 3rd row. → **Median = 2**

No. of Siblings	Frequency	
0	6	**6**
1	11	6 + 11 = 17
2	22	17 + 22 = 39
3	8	
4	2	The 25.5th value is in the group of 2's
5	1	
	50	

Practice questions:

Find the mode and median from the following frequency tables:

a)

No. of Pets	Frequency
0	7
1	5
2	6
3	2
	20

Mode :

Median :

b)

Shoe Size	Frequency
4	2
5	9
6	10
7	4
	25

Mode :

Median :

c)

Age	Frequency
11	6
12	12
13	1
14	7
15	13
16	6

Mode :

Median :

d)

Goals	Frequency
0	6
1	5
2	18
3	12
4	5
5	3

Mode :

Median :

Exam question:

Gary has 60 tubes of smarties.
He counts the number of smarties in each tube.
The table gives information about his results.

a) What is the mode number of smarties in the tubes?

b) What is the median number of smarties in the tubes?

No. of smarties	Frequency
28	9
29	4
30	14
31	15
32	18

(2)

Mean: The mean is found by summing all the values and dividing by the total number of values.
You can use a table to support you in quickly "summing" up all the values.

Example:

Find the mean number of siblings.

Step 1: Create an *fx* column.
Step 2: Calculate the *fx* values by multiplying the columns. (2 x 22 = 44) →
Step 3: Sum the *fx* and frequency columns.
Step 4: Divide the sum of the *fx* column by the sum of the
frequency column.   92 ÷ 50 = 1.84

Mean number of siblings = 1.84

Step 1+2 ↓

No. of Siblings	Frequency	*fx*
0	6	0
1	11	11
2	22	44
3	8	24
4	2	8
5	1	5
Step 3→	50	92

Practice questions:

Calculate the mean of the following sets of data.   **Note:** In exams - column <u>space</u> is usually given

a)

No. of Pets	Frequency	Fx
0	10	
1	6	
2	6	
3	2	

b)

Shoe Size	Frequency	Fx
4	1	
5	3	
6	11	
7	5	

c)

Age	Frequency
11	6
12	12
13	1
14	7
15	13
16	6

d)

Goals	Frequency
0	6
1	5
2	18
3	12
4	5
5	4

Exam question:

Gary has 60 tubes of smarties.
He counts the number of smarties in each tube.
The table gives information about his results.

Calculate the mean number of smarties in the tubes.

No. of smarties	Frequency
28	9
29	4
30	18
31	15
32	14

(3)

Modal class and median class from grouped frequency tables

Modal class: As the data is grouped you can't work out the exact mode, you can only identify the group which has the highest frequency. The **modal class** is the group in the table with the highest frequency.

Example:

Identify the modal class of test scores from the table of results shown:

The interval which has the highest frequency (32) is $30 < x \le 40$.

Modal class = $\mathbf{30 < x \le 40}$

Score in test	Frequency
$0 \le x < 10$	5
$10 \le x < 20$	16
$20 \le x < 30$	21
$30 \le x < 40$	32
$40 \le x < 50$	11
$50 \le x < 60$	15

Median class: The median class is the group that the middle value lies in.
You can find where the middle value lies by adding 1 to the total and dividing by 2.

Example

Identify the median class of test scores from the table shown:

Median position is $(100 + 1) \div 2 = 50.5$.
So the median value is the 50.5th value.
Add up the frequencies until you get to the 50.5th value.
The 50.5th value lies in the 4th row. Median class = $\mathbf{30 \le x \le 40}$

Score in test	Frequency	
$0 \le x < 10$	5	**5**
$10 \le x < 20$	16	**5 + 16 = 21**
$20 \le x < 30$	21	**21 + 21 = 42**
$30 \le x < 40$	32	**42 + 32 = 74**
$40 \le x < 50$	11	The 50.5th value lies
$50 \le x < 60$	15	between 30 and 40

Practice questions:

Find the modal class and median class from the following frequency tables.

a)

No. of Pets	Frequency
$0 \le x < 2$	7
$2 \le x < 4$	2
$4 \le x < 6$	0
$6 \le x < 8$	1

Modal class :

Median class :

b)

Shoe Size	Frequency
$1 \le x < 3$	3
$3 \le x < 5$	9
$5 \le x < 7$	5
$7 \le x < 9$	13

Modal class :

Median class :

c)

Age	Frequency
$0 \le x < 10$	7
$10 \le x < 20$	14
$20 \le x < 30$	15
$30 \le x < 40$	9
$40 \le x < 50$	5
$50 \le x < 60$	7

Modal class :

Median class :

d)

Wins	Frequency
$0 \le x < 6$	11
$6 \le x < 12$	15
$12 \le x < 18$	11
$18 \le x < 24$	19
$24 \le x < 30$	8
$30 \le x < 36$	2

Modal class :

Median class :

Exam question:

40 painters painted a wall. The time they took in minutes was recorded. The table shows the information about their results.

a) Write down the modal class.
b) Find the group containing the median.

Time taken (m mins)	Frequency
$0 < m \le 10$	18
$10 < m \le 20$	13
$20 < m \le 30$	11
$30 < m \le 40$	9
$40 < m \le 50$	9

(2)

Estimating the mean from grouped frequency tables

Mean: As the data is grouped, you can only estimate the mean by using the midpoints of the groups. Once you have found the midpoints, you follow the same process as mean from a frequency table.

Example:

Using the frequency table, estimate the mean test score.

Step 1: Find the midpoints.
You can add the end values and divide by 2. $\frac{20+30}{2} = 25 \rightarrow$

Step 1: Calculate the 'fx' values by multiplying the frequency with the midpoints for each row. $11 \times 45 = 495 \rightarrow$

Step 3: Sum the fx and frequency columns.

Step 4: Divide the sum of the fx column by the sum of the frequency column. $3230 \div 100 = 32.3$

Score in test	Frequency	Midpoints	fx
		Step 1↓	**Step 2↓**
$0 \le x < 10$	5	5	25
$10 \le x < 20$	16	15	240
$20 \le x < 30$	21	25	525
$30 \le x < 40$	32	35	1120
$40 \le x < 50$	11	45	495
$50 \le x < 60$	15	55	825
Step 3→	100	**Step 3→**	3230

Estimated mean score = 32.3

Practice questions:

Calculate an **estimate** for the mean of the following sets of data: **NB:** Table space is usually given

a)

No. of Pets	Frequency	Midpoint	Fx
$0 \le x < 2$	7		
$2 \le x < 4$	2		
$4 \le x < 6$	0		
$6 \le x < 8$	1		

b)

Shoe Size	Frequency	Midpoint	Fx
$1 \le x < 3$	3		
$3 \le x < 5$	8		
$5 \le x < 7$	5		
$7 \le x < 9$	14		

c)

Age	Frequency
$0 \le x < 10$	7
$10 \le x < 20$	14
$20 \le x < 30$	15
$30 \le x < 40$	9
$40 \le x < 50$	5
$50 \le x < 60$	7

d)

Wins	Frequency
$0 \le x < 6$	11
$6 \le x < 12$	15
$12 \le x < 18$	11
$18 \le x < 24$	19
$24 \le x < 30$	8
$30 \le x < 36$	2

📋 Exam question:

40 painters painted a wall.

The time they took in minutes was recorded.

The table shows the results.

Calculate an estimate for mean time taken for painters to paint a standard wall.

Time taken (m mins)	Frequency
$0 < m \le 10$	3
$10 < m \le 20$	8
$20 < m \le 30$	11
$30 < m \le 40$	9
$40 < m \le 50$	9

(4)

Probability – mutually exclusive events

Mutually exclusive events can't happen at the same time. For example: you can't flip a head and a tail on a coin at the same time. The probabilities of mutually exclusive events add up to 1 (certain).

Examples:

a) The probability it will rain tomorrow is 0.8
   What is the probability it won't rain?

These events are mutually exclusive
so the probabilities must add to 1.
The probability it won't rain $= 1 - 0.8 = $ **0.2**

b) The probability John wins a game of snooker is $\frac{3}{11}$
   What is the probability he loses?

These events are mutually exclusive
so the probabilities must add to 1.
The probability it won't rain $= 1 - \frac{3}{11} = \frac{8}{11}$

Practice questions:

Find the probability that it won't rain, if the probability that it will rain is:

a) 0.6 [ ]   c) 0.58 [ ]   e) 0.425 [ ]   g) 0.892 [ ]

b) 0.1 [ ]   d) 0.81 [ ]   f) 0.637 [ ]   h) 0.028 [ ]

Practice questions:

Find the probability that Terry win will at darts, if the probability he loses is:

i) $\frac{1}{2}$ [ ]   k) $\frac{8}{13}$ [ ]   m) $\frac{5}{17}$ [ ]   o) $\frac{13}{123}$ [ ]

j) $\frac{4}{7}$ [ ]   l) $\frac{5}{21}$ [ ]   n) $\frac{36}{77}$ [ ]   p) $\frac{58}{241}$ [ ]

Example:

What is the probability I roll a 5 on the biased dice?

The probabilities must add to 1
$0.1 + 0.3 + 0.25 + 0.15 + 0.05 = 0.85$
The probability of rolling a 5 $= 1 - 0.85 = $ **0.15**

Number	1	2	3	4	5	6
Probability	0.1	0.3	0.25	0.15		0.05

Practice questions:

Find the missing probabilities in the tables below:

q)
Win	Lose	Draw
	0.3	0.1

r)
1	2	3
0.8	0.2	

s)
A	B	C
$\frac{4}{11}$		$\frac{1}{11}$

t)
A	B	C	D	E
	0.37	0.24	0.11	0.25

u)
1	2	3	4	5
0.09	0.1	0.24		0.34

v)
B	G	R	Y	O
$\frac{12}{99}$		$\frac{2}{99}$	$\frac{34}{99}$	$\frac{17}{99}$

w)
A	E	I	O	U
	0.428	0.216	0.124	0.067

x)
1	2	3	4	5	6
0.213	0.156	0.056		0.345	0.108

y)
1	2	3	4	5	6
$\frac{23}{873}$		$\frac{143}{873}$	$\frac{84}{873}$	$\frac{347}{873}$	$\frac{152}{873}$

z) Find the value of x in these tables:

1	2	3	4	5	6
0.33	2x	0.03	x	0.22	0.12

Exam question:

There are only red, white and blue balls in a bag.
There are the same amount of blue balls as white balls.
Complete the table.

Colour	Red	White	Blue
Probability	0.7		

(3)

Probability – OR rule

In probability questions that ask about probabilities of more than one option (OR), you can replace the OR with a plus

If two event are mutually exclusive:
P(A or B) = P(A) + P(B)

Example:

I pick a shape at random from the box.

What is the probability I pick a square or a circle?

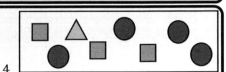

The probability I pick a square is: $\dfrac{3}{8}$ The probability I pick a circle is: $\dfrac{4}{8}$

The probability I pick a square or a circle is: $\dfrac{3}{8} + \dfrac{4}{8} = \dfrac{7}{8}$

Practice questions:

Connor holds 10 playing cards as shown in his hands. Dave selects one card at random.

What is the probability that Dave chooses a:

a) Jack or King?

b) 7 or 8?

c) 6 or 8?

d) even or odd number?

e) diamond ♦ or heart ♥?

f) club ♣ or spade ♠?

g) 2 or 3?

h) 10 or 8?

i) Under 9?

Practice questions:

Juliet has some letter cards that spell MATHS SCHOOL.

She takes one letter at random:

What is the probability that she chooses:

M A T H S S C H O O L

j) A consonant

k) A vowel

l) H or O

m) S, T or L

n) Not an O or L

o) Not an A, S or L

Practice questions:

Romeo rolls a fair six sided dice.

What is the probability that the dices lands on a:

p) 1 or 2

q) 2, 4 or 6

r) odd or even

s) factor of 6

t) multiple of 2

u) square number

Exam question:

Here is a fair 7-sided spinner.

The spinner is to be spun once.

a) What is the probability that it will land on red or white?

b) What is the probability that it does **not** land on green or red?

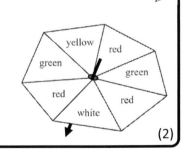

(2)

Probability – AND rule

In probability questions that ask about probabilities of subsequent events, you can replace the AND with a multiply.

If two event are independent:
P(A and B) = P(A) x P(B)

Example:

I pick a shape at random from the box, replace it, and then pick another shape at random. What is the probability I pick a square then a circle?

The probability I pick a square is: $\frac{3}{8}$

The probability I pick a circle is: $\frac{4}{8}$

The probability I pick a square and then a circle is: $\frac{3}{8} \times \frac{4}{8} = \frac{12}{64}$

Practice questions:

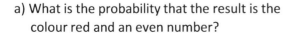

Connor holds 10 playing cards as shown in his hands.

Dave selects one card at random, replaces it, and then chooses another.

What is the probability that the two cards that Dave chooses are:

a) a jack, followed by a king?

d) an odd number, followed by an even number?

b) a 7, followed by an 8?

e) a club followed by a heart?

c) a diamond number, followed by a picture card?

f) a cube number, followed by a spade?

Practice questions:

The probability that Leo scores a goal is 0.7
The probability that Harry scores a goal is 0.6

What is the probability that:

g) both Leo and Harry score?

j) Harry scores and Leo doesn't?

h) neither of them score?

k) only one person scores?

i) Leo scores and Harry doesn't?

l) at least one of them scores?

Exam question:

Here is a fair 7-sided spinner and a fair 6-sided dice.
The spinner is to be spun once and the dice is thrown once.

a) What is the probability that the result is the colour red and an even number?

b) What is the probability it doesn't land on green and 6?

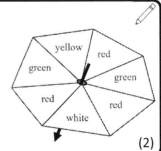

(2)

Venn diagrams

Venn diagrams are used to sort data into groups, and these groups are represented by circles. The area where circles overlap represent where information meets more than one groups criteria.

Example:

50 people were surveyed.
12 of the people like coffee and tea.
21 people like tea.
29 people like coffee.
Complete the Venn diagram.

Always start in the middle of a Venn
Diagram if you can, and work outwards.

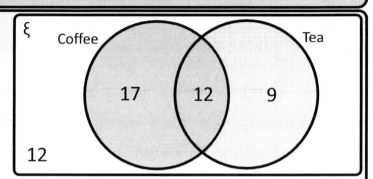

12 people like both so put this in the middle.
21 people like tea so the full tea circle must add to 21. $21 - 12 = \textbf{9}$
29 people like coffee so the full circle must add to 29. $29 - 12 = \textbf{17}$
The rest of the people like neither. $50 - 17 - 12 - 9 = \textbf{12}$

Practice questions:

Complete the Venn diagrams with the values given:

a) 80 people were surveyed.
   42 people like coffee and tea.
   49 people like tea.
   58 people like coffee.

b) 65 people were surveyed.
   18 people like blue and green.
   37 people like blue.
   29 people like green.

c) 40 people were surveyed.
   12 people like fish and chips.
   18 people like fish.
   6 people like neither.

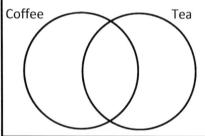

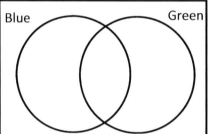

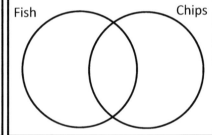

d) 90 people were surveyed.
   24 people like orange and apple.
   48 people like orange.
   30 people like apple.

e) 50 people were surveyed.
   8 people like all 3 drinks.
   11 people like coffee & tea.
   9 people like tea and milk.
   14 people like coffee & milk.
   22 people like coffee.
   24 people like tea.
   17 people like milk.

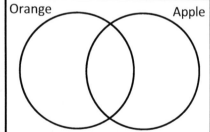

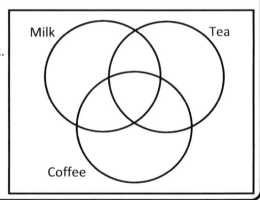

Exam question:

A gym runs two fitness classes, spinning and circuits.
On Saturday 100 people visited the gym.
27 people attended the spinning class.
15 people attended both classes.
50 people did not attend either class.
Represent this information on the Venn diagram.

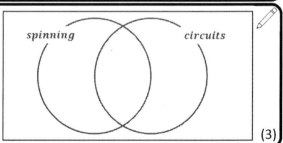

(3)

Venn diagrams (2)

Venn diagrams are used to sort data into groups, and these groups are represented by circles. The area where circles overlap represent where information meets more than one groups criteria.

Example:
50 people were surveyed.
21 people like tea.
29 people like coffee.
12 liked neither
Complete the Venn diagram.

If you are not given the middle group, you need to use the values given to find it.

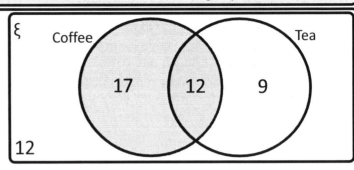

Step 1: Since **12** people liked neither – that can go outside of the circle.
Step 2: Find the middle. Using the total surveyed (50) and the value of that liked neither (12), the values inside the circles must add up to 50 − 12 = 38
Since 29 (coffee) and 21 (tea) add up to 50, this is 12 more than 38, so **12** must be the value in the centre.
Step 3: Find the value for just coffee → 29 − 12 = **17**
Step 4: Find the value for just tea → 21 − 12 = **9**

You can check your solution against the initial values given

Practice questions:
Complete the Venn diagrams with the values given:

a) 48 people were surveyed.
   20 people like orange.
   28 people like apple.
   18 people like neither.

b) 74 people were surveyed.
   45 people like pepper.
   37 people like salt.
   22 people like neither.

c) 100 people were surveyed.
   60 people have a cat.
   55 people have a dog.
   8 people have neither.

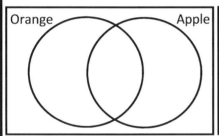
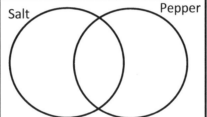
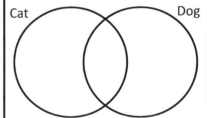

d) 58 people were surveyed.
   24 people have an xBox.
   22 people have a PS4.
   15 people had neither.

e) 100 people were surveyed.
   86 people have a car.
   48 people have a bike.
   12 people have neither.

f) 140 people were surveyed.
   75 people have android.
   80 people have iPhones.
   5 people had neither.

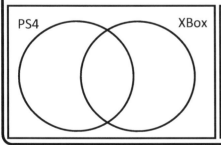
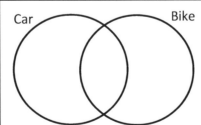
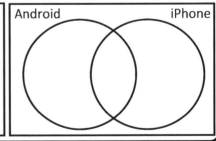

Exam question:
A college run a number of evening classes.
100 people attend the college's evening classes.
28 people attend an Art class.
24 people attend a French class.
51 people do not attend either the Art or French class.
Represent this information on the Venn diagram.

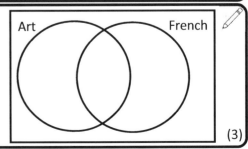

(3)

Venn diagrams: set notation

Set notation is used to list numbers.
ξ represents all the numbers in our Venn diagram.
A = {2,5,7} means the numbers 2, 5 and 7 are in set A.
A $\cap$ B means the numbers that are in **both** set A **and** set B.   (intersection)
A $\cup$ B means the numbers that are in **either** set A **or** set B (**or both**).   (union)
A' means the numbers that are **not** in set A.   (complement)
P(A) = Probability of choosing a number from set A.   n(A) = The number in set A.

Example: ξ = {numbers 1 to 10}   A = {1, 4, 7, 8} B = {2, 4, 8, 9}

Given the set of number shown above, list the members of:

a) A$\cap$B   **{4, 8}** - because these numbers are in both set A <u>and</u> set B.
b) n(A)   **4** – because there are 4 numbers in the set.
c) A$\cup$B   **{1, 2, 4, 7, 8, 9}** - because these numbers are in set A <u>or</u> set B.
d) A'   **{2, 3, 5, 6, 9, 10}** - because these numbers are <u>not</u> in set A.
e) A$\cap$B'   **{1, 7}** - because these numbers are in set A <u>and not</u> in set B.
f) P(B') $\frac{6}{10}$ – because there are 6 numbers not in set B out of 10 in total.

Practice questions:

ξ = {numbers 1 to 10}

A = {1, 3, 5, 7, 9}   B = {2, 3, 4, 5, 6}   C = {3, 6, 8, 9, 10}   D = {1, 2, 4, 7, 10}

Given the set of number shown above, list the members of:

a) A$\cap$B

b) A$\cap$C

c) B$\cup$D

d) D$\cap$A

e) C$\cup$B

f) C$\cap$D

g) A'$\cup$D

h) D$\cap$A'

i) B$\cup$C'

j) C'$\cap$B'

k) C'$\cap$D

l) D'$\cup$C'

Calculate the following probabilities:

m) P(A$\cap$B)

n) P(A$\cup$C)

o) P(B$\cap$D)

p) P(A$\cup$D')

q) P(B$\cap$A')

r) P((A$\cap$B)')

Exam question:

ξ = {1, 2, 3, 4, 5, 6, 7, 8, 9, 10, 11, 12, 13, 14, 15, 16}
A = multiples of 3 and B = multiples of 5

One of the numbers is selected at random.
a) Write down P(A$\cup$B).

b) Write down the list of numbers which represent A'$\cap$B'.

(3)

Venn diagrams: set notation (2)

n(A) = The number in set A.
If this notation is used you must give the number of elements in the set rather than list the elements

Example: ξ = {numbers 1 to 10}   A = {1, 4, 7, 8} B = {2, 4, 8, 9}

Given the set of number shown above, find:
a) n(A)   **4** – because there are 4 numbers in the set.
b) n(A∪B)   **6** – because there are 6 numbers in set A or set B: {1, 2, 4, 7, 8, 9}
c) n((A∩B)')   **8** – because there are 8 numbers that are <u>not</u> in set A <u>and</u> set B: {1, 2, 3, 5, 6, 7, 9, 10}

Practice questions:

ξ = {numbers 1 to 10}   A = {1, 2, 6, 8, 9}   B = {2, 3, 5, 6, 7, 8}   C = {4, 8, 10}   D = {1, 3, 5, 7, 10}

Given the set of number shown above, find:

a) n(A)

b) n(C)

c) n(A∩B)

d) n(C∩D)

e) n(B')

f) n(B∪C)

g) n(A∩D)'

h) n(B∪D')

If an element is contained in a set you use the notation: ∈
If an element is **not** contained in a set you use the notation: ∉

Example: A = {1, 2, 7}
a) Is 4 ∈ A?   No because 4 is not in set A.   b) Is 2 ∈ A?   Yes because 2 is in set A.Z

Practice questions: A = {1, 2, 3}   B = {4, 6, 7, 9}
True or False?

i) 3 ∈ A

j) 2 ∈ B

k) 1 ∉ A

l) 8 ∉ B

m) 9 ∈ B

n) 4 ∉ A

A subset is a set where all the elements are members of another set.
A ⊂ B means set A is a subset of set B   A ⊄ B means set A is **not** a subset of set B
If all the elements of set A are exactly the same as all the elements in set B then set A is still a subset of B
but it is not a 'proper subset'.

Example: A = {1, 2, 7} B = {2, 5, 8} C = {1, 2, 4, 5, 7, 9}
a) Is A ⊂ C?   Yes because all the elements of set A are contained in set C.
b) Is B ⊂ C?   No because set B contains 8 which is not in set C.

Practice questions:

A = {1, 3}   B = {4, 7}   C = {2, 4, 6, 8, 10}   D = {1, 2, 3, 4, 5}   E = {1, 3, 4, 5, 7, 8}   F = {1, 3}

True or False?

o) A ⊂ D

p) B ⊂ C

q) A ⊄ B

r) B ⊄ E

s) A ⊂ F

t) E ⊂ A

u) A ⊂ E

v) E ⊄ B

w) D ⊄ C

Venn diagrams: shading regions

Set notation can used to highlight regions on Venn diagrams.
A ∩ B means the numbers that are in **both** set A **and** set B.   (intersection)
A ∪ B means the numbers that are in **either** set A **or** set B (**or both**).   (union)
A' means the numbers that are **not** in set A.   (complement)

Example:

Shade in the region that represents A∩B.

a) A∩B   **Step 1)** Mark the regions A.   ☆
    Step 2) Mark the regions B.   ☾
    Step 3) Mark the region that satisfy both A **and** B.
    Step 4) Shade the regions marked with both.

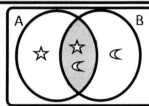

b) A ∪ B'   **Step 1)** Mark the regions A.   ☆
    Step 2) Mark the regions B'.   ☀
    Step 2) Mark the region that satisfy both A **or** B'.
    Step 3) Shade the regions marked with either symbol.

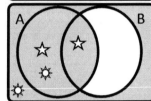

Practice questions:

Shade the region on the Venn diagrams which represents:

a) B∩A

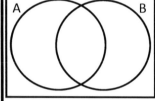

b) A'

c) A∪B

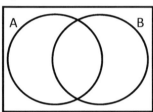

d) A'∩B

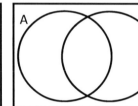

e) A∩B'

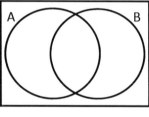

f) A'∪B

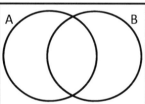

g) A'∩B'

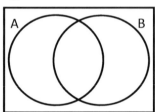

h) A'∪B'

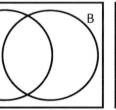

i) (A∩B)'

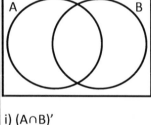

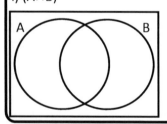

j) (A'∩B)'

k) (A∪B')'

l) (A∪B)'

Exam question:

A and B are two sets shown in the Venn diagram.

a) Shade the region which represents A∩B'.

b) If n(A) = 70
    n(A ∩ B') = 40
    n(B) = 50
    Find n(B ∩ A')

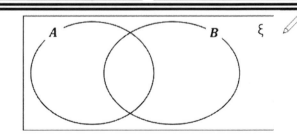

(3)

Probabilities from Venn diagrams

P(A) means what is the probability a number is in set A.

Example:
A number is chosen at random, find:

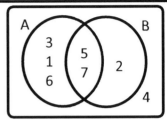

a) P(A)   There are 5 members of set A (3, 1, 6, 5, 7)

          There are 7 members altogether

          $P(A) = \frac{5}{7}$

b) P(A∩B)   There are 2 members of set A∩B (5, 7)

            There are 7 members altogether $P(A∩B) = \frac{2}{7}$

Practice questions:

A number is chosen at random, find:

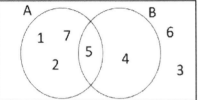

a) P(A)

b) P(B)

c) P(A')

d) P(A∩B)

e) P(B')

f) P(A∪B)

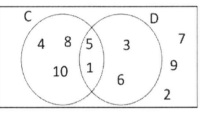

g) P(C)

h) P(C∩D)

i) P(C∪D)

j) P(C'∩D)

k) P(C∩D')

l) P(C'∩D')

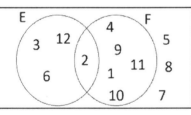

m) P(E'∩F)

n) P(E'∪F)

o) P(E∪F')

p) P(E'∩F')

q) P(E∩F')

r) P(E'∪F')

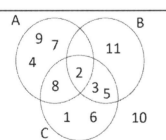

s) P(A∩B∩C)

t) P(B∩C)

u) P(A∪C)

v) P(A∪B∪C)

w) P(A'∩B∩C)

x) P(A∪B∪C')

Exam question:

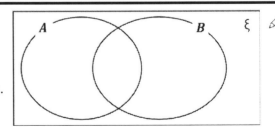

ξ = {even numbers between 1 and 21}
A = {2, 6, 8, 12, 20}   B = {4, 6, 10, 12, 14}

a) Complete the Venn diagram to show the information.

A number is chosen at random from the universal set ξ.
b) What is P(A∪B)?

(4)

131

Page 1-2:
a) 20.25 b) 0.57142857... c) 0.049382716... d) 11.6523 e) 3.18181818... f) 0.1710512892...
g) 0.4226182617... h) 0.7660444431... i) 0.3639702343... j) 84.28940686... k) 53.13010235...
l) 11.53695903... m) 0.935414346... n) 2.182879407... o) 2.692793703... p) 1.242118007...
q) -0.218880868... r) 1.605285203... s) 3.932370045... t) 31.60293922... u) -3.037337381...
v) 5.120413549... w) 1.137675574 x) 0.5469695824...

Exam question: a) 7.527726527... b) 7.53

Page 3:
a) $\frac{5}{7}$ b) $\frac{3}{4}$ c) $\frac{13}{15}$ d) $\frac{5}{6}$ e) $\frac{19}{28}$ f) $1\frac{5}{21}$ g) $1\frac{17}{24}$ h) $1\frac{9}{35}$ i) $\frac{2}{7}$ j) $\frac{5}{8}$ k) $\frac{1}{10}$ l) $\frac{7}{12}$ m) $\frac{4}{35}$ n) $\frac{8}{21}$ o) $-\frac{3}{10}$ p) $-\frac{5}{28}$

Exam question: $\frac{4}{15}$

Page 4:
a) $3\frac{4}{5}$ b) 7 c) $5\frac{1}{3}$ d) $3\frac{5}{6}$ e) $3\frac{19}{35}$ f) $4\frac{37}{42}$ g) $3\frac{7}{40}$ h) $10\frac{11}{72}$ i) $3\frac{1}{6}$ j) 4
k) $1\frac{11}{14}$ l) $\frac{3}{28}$ m) $2\frac{22}{35}$ n) $\frac{35}{66}$ o) $-\frac{23}{24}$ p) $-5\frac{11}{36}$

Exam question: $15\frac{11}{15}$

Page 5:
a) $\frac{6}{49}$ b) $\frac{1}{8}$ c) $\frac{2}{15}$ d) $\frac{3}{28}$ e) $\frac{8}{21}$ f) $\frac{5}{8}$ g) $\frac{2}{3}$ h) $\frac{1}{3}$ i) $\frac{5}{6}$ j) $1\frac{2}{3}$ k) 6 l) $1\frac{1}{4}$ m) $3\frac{1}{3}$ n) $1\frac{4}{21}$ o) $\frac{4}{9}$ p) $1\frac{1}{2}$ q) $\frac{5}{12}$ r) $3\frac{1}{2}$ s) $2\frac{2}{5}$ t) $\frac{11}{14}$ u) $1\frac{1}{20}$

Exam question: $16\frac{7}{8}$ km

Page 6:
a) £12.80 b) £64 c) £36 d) £9.60 e) £519.40 f) £14.95 g) £5.46 h) £812.16 i) £511.42 j) £1.02
k) £36 l) £132 m) £78 n) £75 o) £133.40 p) £96.30 q) £40.32 r) £111.87 s) £79.20 t) £108.64
u) £8 v) £25.20 w) £72 x) £90 y) £50.32 z) £27.60 α) £22.40 β) £52.54 γ) £15.51 δ) £23.94

Page 7:
a) 10% b) 10% c) 100% d) 30% e) 30% f) 64% g) 6% h) 47% i) 11% j) 21.9% k) 50% l) 25%
m) 30% n) 95% o) 70% p) 28% q) 45% r) 12% s) 62% t) 2.15%

Exam question: 22%

Page 8:
a) £266.20 b) £288 c) £491.72 d) £128.73 e) £191.95 f) £657.73 g) 25 years h) 12 years

Exam question: £42,668.48

Page 9:
a) £352895.40 b) £389328.93 c) £486895.11 d) £780530.28 e) £23619.60 f) £17909.82
g) £15925.25 h) £18899.50

Exam question: 6 years

Page 10:
a) £60 b) £30 c) £50 d) £40 e) £120 f) £64 g) £23 h) £70 i) £48 j) £80 k) £130 l) £240 m) £148
n) £45.50

Exam question: 75

Solutions

Page 11:

a) 2^6 b) 3^7 c) 6^{10} d) x^7 e) 8^7 f) 2^5 g) 9^3 h) 2^{-4} i) 5^{-2} j) x^{-3} k) $4^0 = 1$ l) 7^{-9} m) x^{-7} n) 2^5 o) y^{-4}
p) 2^2 q) 3^3 r) 6^6 s) x t) 8^5 u) 2^{-9} v) 9^{-11} w) 2^{-12} x) 5^6 y) x^{13} z) 4^4 α) 7^{-1} β) x^3 γ) 2^5 δ) y^4

Exam question: $a^3 b^4 c^3$

Page 12:

a) 2^{10} b) 5^{21} c) 3^{18} d) 8^6 e) 2^{-10} f) 4^{-12} g) 6^{-6} h) 9^{-6} i) $3^0 = 1$ j) 4^{-16} k) 7^4 l) $5^0 = 1$
m) $\frac{4}{25}$ n) $\frac{9}{16}$ o) $\frac{25}{36}$ p) $\frac{16}{49}$ q) $\frac{1}{27}$ r) $\frac{1}{16}$ s) $1\frac{7}{9}$ t) $2\frac{1}{4}$ u) $3\frac{1}{16}$ v) $5\frac{1}{16}$ w) $12\frac{1}{4}$ x) $37\frac{1}{27}$

Exam question: $\frac{1}{18}$

Page 13:

a) $28a^7 b^{12}$ b) $45x^{11}y^9$ c) $24p^6 q^{17}$ d) $24x^{14}y^{10}$ e) $49a^{16}b^2$ f) $52p^8 q^6$ g) $24x^3 y^8$ h) $56a^{17}b^4$
i) $42x^{-6}y^5$ j) $4x^4 y^3$ k) $8x^7 y^7$ l) $4ab^4$ m) $10y^4$ n) $4x^5 y^3$ o) $6b^{-3}c^6$ p) $7y^{-6}$ q) $6v^{-3}w^{-1}$
r) $8x^{-11}y^9$ s) $36x^8 y^{14}$ t) $25a^{16}b^2$ u) $8x^{27}y^6$ v) $81g^6 h^{16}$ w) $27m^3 n^{15}$ x) $16x^{24}y^{44}$ y) $125x^{-12}y^{36}$
z) $64a^2 b^8 c^{-18}$ α) $32x^{60}y^{35}z^5$

Exam question: $6x^{-2}y^{11}$ or $\frac{6y^{11}}{x^2}$

Page 14:

a) $\frac{1}{64}$ b) $\frac{1}{32}$ c) $\frac{1}{7}$ d) $\frac{1}{125}$ e) $\frac{1}{36}$ f) $\frac{1}{81}$ g) $\frac{1}{9}$ h) $\frac{1}{216}$ i) $\frac{1}{4}$ j) $\frac{1}{16}$ k) 1 l) $\frac{1}{81}$ m) $\frac{1}{y^2}$ n) $\frac{1}{d^4}$ o) $\frac{1}{x}$ p) $\frac{1}{p^3}$ q) $\frac{1}{k^7}$
r) $\frac{1}{h^2}$ s) $\frac{1}{z^8}$ t) $\frac{1}{y}$ u) $\frac{1}{c^5}$ v) $\frac{1}{9y^2}$ w) $\frac{1}{49x^2}$ x) $\frac{3}{t^3}$ y) $\frac{1}{64y^3}$ z) $\frac{5}{x^2}$ α) $\frac{1}{25x^2}$ β) $\frac{9}{x^5}$ γ) $\frac{1}{216y^3}$ δ) $\frac{8}{x^2}$

Exam question: i) x^{12} ii) $\frac{1}{a^3}$

Page 15:

a) $2^3 \times 3$ b) $2 \times 3 \times 5$ c) $2^3 \times 5$ d) 3^3 e) $2 \times 5 \times 7$ f) $2^2 \times 3^3$ g) $2^3 \times 7$ h) $2^2 \times 3 \times 11$ **Exam question:** $2^5 \times 5^2$

Page 16-17:

a) HCF = 6 LCM = 120 b) HCF = 3 LCM = 165 c) HCF = 4 LCM = 220 d) HCF = 8 LCM = 160
e) HCF = 18 LCM = 216 f) HCF = 8 LCM = 1056 g) HCF = 4 LCM = 2128 h) HCF = 2 LCM = 7592
i) HCF = 8 LCM = 2760 j) HCF = 2 LCM = 720 k) HCF = 7 LCM = 210

Exam question: a) $2^4 \times 3$ b) 528

Page 18:

a) HCF = 300 LCM = 162000 b) HCF = 1296 LCM = 762048 c) HCF = 15435 LCM = 5942475
d) HCF = 686 LCM = 86436000 e) HCF = 4056 LCM = 146016 f) HCF = 15435 LCM = 8022341250

Exam question: a) 45375 b) 2223601875

Page 19:

a) HCF = 1250 LCM = 250000 b) HCF = 1029 LCM = 9529569 c) HCF = 180 LCM = 1944000
d) HCF = 2205 LCM = 3472875 e) HCF = 66 LCM = 1254528 f) HCF = 2450 LCM = 6860000

Exam question: a) $3^2 \times 5^{23}$ b) 3×5^{28}

Page 20:

a) 1:5 b) 1:7 c) 1:4.5 d) 1:0.5 e) 1:0.4 f) 1:1.5 g) 1:4.8 h) 1:3:4.5 i) 1:0.888... j) 100g butter
k) 25g butter l) 5g butter m) 15g butter n) 70ml milk o) 14ml milk p) 98ml milk q) 392ml milk
r) 25 s) 8 t) 35 u) 22

Exam question: a) 300g b) 50

Page 21:
a) 5 pens for 90p (18p each) b) 6 chocolate bars for £8 (£1.33 each) c) 5 bottles of wine for £29 (5.80 each) d) 32 sweets for £4.34 (13.56p each) e) 20 hours f) 15 hours g) 15 hours
Exam question: 8 cupcakes for £6 (75p each)

Page 22:
a) 2:3 b) 5:3 c) 1:3 d) 10:7 e) 3:5 f) 5:7 g) 1:3 h) 8:9 i) 15:13 j) 14:11 k) 5:3:6 l) 3:5:7 m) £4, £16
n) £6, £14 o) £12, £20 p) £24, £8 q) £40, £8 r) £28, £20 s) £60, £140 t) £45, £27 u) £22, £44, £66
v) £41, £82, £82
Exam question: 5:2

Page 23:
a) £36 b) £30 c) £44 d) £96 e) 40,000 f) 13,000 g) 6,500 h) 9,000 i) 3,300
Exam question: 32

Page 24:
a) $\frac{7}{9}$ b) $\frac{8}{13}$ c) $\frac{9}{16}$ d) $\frac{1}{9}$ e) $\frac{6}{11}$ f) $\frac{5}{11}$ g) $\frac{11}{20}$ h) $\frac{13}{28}$ i) $\frac{6}{23}$ j) $\frac{14}{19}$ k) $\frac{27}{46}$ l) $\frac{31}{38}$ m) $\frac{7}{15}$ n) $\frac{9}{15}$ or $\frac{3}{5}$ o) $\frac{11}{13}$ p) $\frac{9}{16}$ q) $\frac{4}{17}$
r) $\frac{11}{20}$ s) $\frac{6}{19}$ t) $\frac{15}{23}$ u) $\frac{14}{15}$ v) $\frac{19}{36}$ w) $\frac{15}{43}$ x) $\frac{32}{55}$ y) $\frac{5}{15}$ or $\frac{1}{3}$ z) $\frac{5}{15}$ or $\frac{1}{3}$ α) $\frac{2}{23}$ β) $\frac{5}{20}$ or $\frac{1}{4}$ γ) $\frac{2}{16}=\frac{1}{8}$ δ) $\frac{7}{20}$ ε) $\frac{11}{40}$
μ) $\frac{10}{44}=\frac{5}{22}$ π) $\frac{15}{35}=\frac{3}{7}$ **Exam question:** $\frac{11}{19}$

Page 25:
a) 8:3 b) 3:20 c) 36:7 d) 10:3 e) 27:5 f) 400 g) 1800 h) 480   **Exam question:** 222

Page 26:
Set 1: a) 5 b) 8 c) 40 d) 0.03 e) 30 f) 0.8 g) 700 h) 0.06 i) 7000 j) 2 k) 20000 l) 500
  m) 80 n) 4000 o) 0.005 p) 200
Set 2: a) 2.6 b) 0.78 c) 790 d) 12.71 e) 1100 f) 5800 g) 80 h) 0.40 i) 5000 j) 6800
  k) 0.51 l) 0.034 m) 46 n) 6.9 o) 3.0 p) 4000
Set 3: a) 43400 b) 701 c) 6750 d) 0.00454 e) 0.551 f) 0.0701 g) 60800 h) 0.490 i) 40.0
Exam question: a) 3.1 b) 3.141593

Page 27:
a) 150 b) 2000 c) 5 d) 2400000 e) 20 f) 980 g) 25.5 h) 1.5 i) 40 j) 30 k) 25 l) 100 m) 1200
n) 1000 o) 32000 p) 0.007 q) 0.02 r) 88
Exam question: £24

Page 28: (UB = Upper Bounds and LB = Lower Bound)
a) LB = 5.5, UB = 6.5   b) LB = 17.5, UB = 18.5   c) LB = 19.5, UB = 20.5   d) LB = 87.5, UB = 88.5
e) LB = 2.5, UB = 3.5   f) LB = 10.5, UB = 11.5   g) LB = 53.5, UB = 54.5   h) LB = 99.5, UB = 100.5
i) LB = 3.35, UB = 3.45   j) LB = 7.15, UB = 7.25   k) LB = 11.45, UB = 11.55   l) LB = 13.55, UB = 13.65
m) LB = 18.75, UB = 18.85 n) LB = 5.95, UB = 6.05 o) LB = 6.5, UB = 7.5   p) LB = 8.5, UB = 9.5
q) LB = 25, UB = 35   r) LB = 75, UB = 85   s) LB = 450, UB = 550 t) LB = 50, UB = 150
u) LB = 0.85, UB = 0.95   v) LB = 6500, UB = 7500
Exam question: Lower Bounds = 4.5m and 2.5m → Perimeter = 4.5+4.5+2.5+2.5 = 14m

Page 29:
a) 3×10^2 b) 7×10^2 c) 2×10^3 d) 7.2×10^2 e) 9×10^3 f) 5.4×10^3 g) 3.4×10^4 h) 6.5×10^4 i) 5.32×10^5
j) 5.05×10^5 k) 7.0503×10^6 l) 5.8001×10^7 m) 5×10^{-2} n) 8×10^{-3} o) 5.6×10^{-1} p) 8.6×10^{-3} 5.23×10^{-3}
r) 2.08×10^{-2} s) 9×10^{-6} t) 5.01×10^{-4} u) 4.2×10^{-5} v) 8×10^{-7} w) 1.15×10^{-4} x) 1.0005×10^{-4}
Exam question: a) 5.46×10^8 b) 3.81×10^{-7}

Solutions

Page 30:
a) 2.4×10^5 b) 6.2×10^6 c) 2.67×10^7 d) 3.22×10^5 e) 7.32×10^4 f) 4.43×10^8 g) 8×10^9 h) 3×10^2
i) 2.8×10^7 j) 4×10^2 k) 8.64×10^{13} l) 1.296×10^{14}

Exam question: 4.1×10^3

Page 31:
a) \$65 b) €224 c) ¥5720 d) 11220 Rand e) 45043.20 Rupees f) £400 g) £44.64 h) £34.97 i) £7.46
j) £ 46.52   k) €344.62 l) ¥38303.57 m) UK (by \$1.30 or £1) n) France (by €4.48 or £4)
o) Mexico (by ₱10.55 or £0.43) p) UK (by \$1.64 or £1.26)

Exam question: USA (by \$0.49 or £0.37)

Page 32:
a) 30 b) 11 c) 4 d) 3 e) 4 f) 44 g) 2 h) 36 i) 66 j) 4 k) 38 l) 4 m) 22 n) 43 o) 18 p) -8 q) -6
r) -2 s) 12 t) 26 u) 4 v) -10 w) -16 x) -2 y) -3 z) 56 Δ) 192

Exam question: a) 30°C b) -10°C

Page 33:
a) $C = 6p + 2q$ b) $A = 8p + 2c$ c) $K = 5b + 3s$ d) $J = 60n + 150w$ e) $T = 4.5s + 1.5c$
f) $F = 0.8r + 1.1s$ g) $P = 3a + 1.5b + 2.5c$ h) $C = 0.8x + 1.2y + 3.7z$ i) $P = 7y - 3x$
j) $X = 9.6d - 4.5c$

Page 34:
a) $7x + 27$ b) $7x + 22$ c) $9x - 24$ d) $15x + 54$ e) $47x - 10$ f) $-x - 1$ g) $-2x + 18$ h) $5x - 26$
i) $-8x + 62$ j) $x + 21$ k) $23x - 50$ l) $3x + 66$ m) $12x - 44$ n) $5x + 33$ o) $-8x - 7$

Exam question: $2x - 50$

Page 35:
a) $5(x + 1)$ b) $6(k - 5)$ c) $5(3h + 5)$ d) $7(2a - 7)$ e) $10(2 + y)$ f) $4(6x + 5)$ g) $9(3a + b)$
h) $5(4x - 9y)$ i) $9(8x + 3)$ j) $12(5y - 12)$ k) $12(k - 36m)$ l) $6(3a + 4p)$ m) $8(8x - 9y)$
n) $7(2a + b - 3c)$ o) $5(x + 2y - 3z)$ p) $3x(x + 1)$ q) $6k(k^2 - 4k)$ r) $5x(4 + y)$ s) $8a(4a + b)$
t) $12x^2(2x - 3)$ u) $4x(6x + 5y)$ v) $9a^2(3a + 2)$ w) $4x(7x + 11)$ x) $5x(x - 4 + 2y)$
y) $10a(2ab + 1 - 5bc)$

Exam question: $4x(3x - 8)$

Page 36:
a) $6a^5b^2(3 + 4bc^4)$ b) $3p^3q^3(2p^2qr^2 - 9)$ c) $30a^2b(b^2c^5 + 4a^2)$ d) $18m^3n(2n^3 - 3m^2p^2)$
e) $20rs^4(r^2 + 2s)$ f) $6a^3bc(2a - 9bc^2)$ g) $2n^5pq(3 - 10p^3q^2)$ h) $16st(v^4 + 2s^2t)$
i) $5k^3m(5m^3 - 4)$ j) $3c^4d(3d^2 + 4)$ k) $2v^5wx^2(w^3 + 4x^2)$ l) $7wx^3(2w^3y^5 + 7x)$
m) $12s^2t^4(2 + 3s^3t)$ n) $7x^2y(5 + 4x^3y^2)$ o) $2rst^3(2r^3 - 5st^2)$
p) $6hk^2(k + 3h)$ q) $10p^3q^4(5r^4 - 8p^2q)$ r) $3b^2c(4b^3 + c^3d)$ s) $7d^2e^3f^5(5d^2 + 9e^2)$
t) $7v^3w^2(vw^2 - 12x^4)$

Exam question: $12xy^6z^4(3 - 2x^3y)$

Page 37:
a) $x = 3$ b) $x = 3$ c) $x = 7$ d) $x = 9$ e) $x = 23$ f) $x = 12$ g) $x = 4$ h) $x = 3$ i) $x = 8$ j) $x = 7$ k) $x = -7$
l) $x = -2$ **Exam question:** $x = 6$

Page 38:
a) $x = 3$ b) $x = 1$ c) $x = 2$ d) $x = 4$ e) $x = 3$ f) $x = 5$ g) $x = 6$ h) $x = 7$ i) $x = 6$ j) $x = 3$ k) $x = 2$ l) $x = 3$

Exam question: $x = 8$

Solutions

Page 39:
a) $x = \pm 2$ b) $x = \pm 8$ c) $x = \pm 10$ d) $x = \pm 11$ e) $x = \pm 9$ f) $x = \pm 15$ g) $x = \pm 5$ h) $x = \pm 2$ i) $x = \pm 4$
j) $x = \pm 9$ k) $x = \pm 3$ l) $x = \pm 12$ m) $x = \pm 2$ n) $x = \pm 8$ o) $x = \pm 3$ p) $x = \pm 6$ q) $x = \pm 4$ r) $x = \pm 9$
s) $x = \pm 3$ t) $x = \pm 50$

Exam question: $x = 7$ (positive only as a length cannot be negative)

Page 40:
a) $x = 6$ b) $x = 7$ c) $x = 29$ d) $x = 24$ e) $x = -2$ f) $x = 4$ g) $x = 8$ h) $x = -2$ i) $x = 6$ j) $x = -12$
k) $x = 3$ l) $x = 6$ m) $x = 3$ n) $x = -7$ o) $x = 8$

Exam question: $x = 9$

Page 41:
a) $x = 16$ b) $x = 2$ c) $x = 6$ d) $x = 7$ e) $x = 10$ f) $x = 7$ g) $x = 7$ h) $x = 8$ i) $x = 4$ j) $x = 10$
k) $x = 10$ l) $x = 4$ m) $x = -8$ n) $x = -38$ o) $x = -12$

Exam question: $x = 2$

Page 42:
a) $x = 6$ b) $x = 12$ c) $x = 2$ d) $x = -\frac{1}{3}$ e) $x = -\frac{5}{22}$ f) $x = -\frac{2}{3}$ g) $x = -1$ h) $x = 1$ i) $x = -\frac{1}{18}$
j) $x = \frac{17}{41}$ k) $x = \frac{5}{17}$ l) $x = 14$

Exam question: $x = 35$

Page 43:
a) $x = 3$ b) $x = 14$ c) $x = -15$ d) $x = -4$ e) $x = -10$ f) $x = \frac{5}{2}$ g) $x = 3$ h) $x = 4$ i) $x = \frac{1}{7}$
j) $x = 3$ k) $x = \frac{12}{5}$ l) $x = -\frac{5}{21}$

Exam question: $x = 10$

Page 44:
a) 32 b) 18 c) 22 d) 156 e) 39 f) 83

Exam question: 27

Page 45:

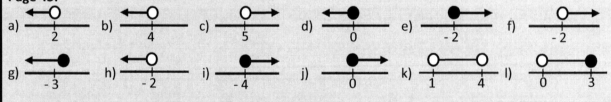

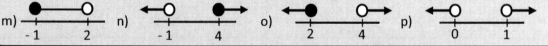

Page 46:
a) $x > 2$ b) $-3 \leq x < 3$ c) $x \leq -1$ d) $x \geq -4$ e) $-5 < x < 0$ f) $-2 < x \leq 6$ g) $x > 1$
h) $-5 \leq x \leq 5$ i) $x \leq 4$ j) $-1 \leq x < 2$ k) $x > 0$ l) $-6 < x < 4$

Page 47:
a) $x \geq 1$ b) $x < 5$ c) $x \leq -2$ d) $x \geq 3$ e) $x > 2$ f) $x \leq 3$ g) $x \leq -3$ h) $x < -\frac{1}{3}$ i) $x > 12$ j) $x \geq 2$
k) $x < 4$ l) $x \leq 9$ m) $x \geq \frac{17}{9}$ n) $x > 8$ o) $x \geq -6$ p) $x \leq 2$ q) $x < -6$ r) $x < 25$

Exam question: 21, 22, 23

Solutions

Page 48:

a) $5 < x < 10$ b) $9 < x \leq 22$ c) $3 \leq x \leq 7$ d) $-11 \leq x < -1$ e) $5 < x \leq 9$ f) $-1 < x < 10$

g) $-4 \leq x < 8$ h) $-\frac{3}{4} \leq x \leq \frac{26}{4}$ i) ←○ over 4 j) ○—● over -3, -1 k) ●→ over -1 l) ←● over -3

m) ●—○ over -4, 2 n) ○→ over -2 o) ●—○ over 0, 3 p) ←○ over -3

Page 49:

a) $x^2 + 6x + 8$ b) $x^2 + 8x + 15$ c) $x^2 + 7x + 6$ d) $x^2 + 14x + 40$ e) $x^2 + 10x + 25$ f) $x^2 + 12x + 27$
g) $x^2 + 6x + 9$ h) $x^2 + 9x + 20$ i) $x^2 - 2x - 8$ j) $x^2 + 2x - 15$ k) $x^2 + 5x - 6$ l) $x^2 - 4x - 5$
m) $x^2 - 25$ n) $x^2 + 6x - 27$ o) $a^2 - 2a - 8$ p) $a^2 + 6a - 7$

Exam question: $x^2 + 9x + 14$

Page 50:

a) $x^2 - 6x + 8$ b) $x^2 - 8x + 15$ c) $x^2 - 7x + 6$ d) $x^2 - 14x + 40$ e) $x^2 - 10x + 25$ f) $x^2 - 11x + 24$
g) $x^2 - 6x + 9$ h) $x^2 - 9x + 20$ i) $2x^2 - 6x - 8$ j) $6x^2 + x - 15$ k) $8x^2 + 22x - 6$ l) $3x^2 - 2x - 5$
m) $4x^2 - 25$ n) $3x^2 - 27$ o) $12a^2 - 22a + 8$ p) $6a^2 - 13a + 6$

Exam question: $6x^2 - 24$

Page 51:

a) $(x + 1)(x + 2)$ b) $(x + 2)(x + 5)$ c) $(x + 2)(x + 6)$ d) $(x + 4)(x + 6)$ e) $(a + 1)(a + 7)$ f) $(x + 1)(x + 9)$
g) $(p + 2)(p + 10)$ h) $(x + 5)(x - 1)$ i) $(y + 4)(y - 2)$ j) $(x - 3)(x - 5)$ k) $(x + 7)(x - 3)$ l) $(x + 3)(x - 7)$
m) $(x + 6)(x + 7)$ n) $(x - 5)(x - 5)$ o) $(k - 1)(k - 4)$ p) $(x + 5)(x - 6)$ q) $(x + 5)(x - 7)$ r) $(x - 2)(x - 12)$
s) $(x - 6)(x - 7)$ t) $(e + 14)(e - 3)$

Exam question: $(x + y)(x + z)$

Page 52:

a) $x = -1$ or $x = -2$ b) $x = -2$ or $x = -5$ c) $x = -2$ or $x = -6$ d) $x = -4$ or $x = -6$ e) $x = 1$ or $x = -2$ f) $x = 2$ or $x = -5$ g) $x = 3$ or $x = -7$ h) $x = -6$ or $x = -7$ i) $x = 5$ j) $x = 1$ or $x = 4$ k) $x = 6$ or $x = -5$ l) $x = 7$ or $x = -5$

Exam question: $x = -3$ or $x = -6$

Page 53:

a) $y = x - 2$ b) $y = x + 3$ c) $y = 2x - 5$ d) $y = 4x$ e) $y = 3x$ f) $y = 2x + 1$ g) $y = 7x$ h) $y = 5x$

i) $y = 2x - 2$ j) $y = \frac{x-5}{2}$ k) $y = \frac{x+3}{5}$ l) $y = \frac{2x-5}{4}$ m) $y = 4x - 2$ n) $y = 3x - 1$ o) $y = 10x$

p) $y = \frac{7x}{2}$ q) $y = 5x - 10$ r) $y = 2x - 1$

Exam question: $a = \frac{v-u}{t}$

Page 54:

a) $x = \sqrt{y}$ b) $x = \sqrt[3]{t}$ c) $x = \sqrt[5]{a}$ d) $x = y^2$ e) $x = w^4$ f) $x = u^3$ g) $x = \sqrt{y - 5}$ h) $x = \sqrt{\frac{t}{3}}$

i) $x = \sqrt{4y}$ j) $x = \sqrt{y + 9}$ k) $x = \sqrt{\frac{y-2}{2}}$ l) $x = \sqrt{\frac{a+4}{b}}$ m) $x = \sqrt{3(y - w)}$ n) $x = \sqrt{25y}$ o) $x = \sqrt{\frac{2}{y}}$

Exam question: $\sqrt{\frac{2s}{a}} = t$

Page 55:

a) $x = 3, y = 2$ b) $x = 1, y = 5$ c) $x = 4, y = 4$ d) $x = 2, y = 7$ e) $x = 2, y = 4$ f) $x = -2, y = 3$
g) $x = 6, y = -3$ h) $x = 5, y = 5$

Page 56:
a) $x = 1, y = 6$ b) $x = 5, y = 2$ c) $x = 7, y = 0$ d) $x = -1, y = 6$ e) $x = 6, y = 2$ f) $x = 0, y = 4$
g) $x = 8, y = 1$ h) $x = 4, y = -4$

Page 57:
a) $x = 2, y = 9$ b) $x = 5, y = -5$ c) $x = -1, y = -4$ d) $x = -1, y = -2$ e) $x = 4, y = 2$ f) $x = 1, y = 8$
g) $x = -3, y = -1$ h) $x = -2, y = 6$
Exam question: Adult: £18, Child: £11

Page 58:
a) $x = 4, y = 5$ b) $x = 2, y = 2$ c) $x = 3, y = 9$ d) $x = 1, y = 5$ e) $x = 5, y = 9$ f) $x = 6, y = 7$ g) $x = 7, y = 5$
h) $x = 10, y = 2$

Page 59:
a) 36° b) 40° c) 65° d) 16.5° e) 38° f) 70° g) 55° h) 30° i) 90° j) 25°
Exam question: $x = 35°$

Page 60:
a) 2cm b) 7cm c) 5cm d) 4cm e) 2cm f) 16cm
Exam question: 4cm

Page 61:
a) 5, 7, 9, 104 b) 3, 9, 15, 300 c) 7, 11, 15, 205 d) 1, 7, 13, 298 e) -1, -9, -17, -397 f) -12, -22, -32, -507
g) 4 , 12 , 28 , 103 h) 2, 18 , 50 , 200 i) 4 , 18 , 40 , 130 j) -1 , 3 , 15 , 80 k) -1 , 1 , 11 , 71
l) -2 , 20 , 58, 2233
Exam question: $2(10)^2 + 4(10) - 1 = 239$

Page 62:
a) 12, 20, 28, 36, 44 b) -1, 2, 5, 8, 11 c) 19, 13, 7, 1, -5 d) 3, 12, 27, 48, 75 e) 2, 9, 18, 29, 42
f) -2, 6, 24, 52, 90 g) $2n + 1$ h) $4n - 2$ i) $5n + 2$ j) $4n - 4$ k) $8n - 7$ l) $6n - 2$ m) $12n - 10$ n) $5n - 13$
o) $-2n + 18$ p) $-5n + 7$
Exam question: a) $3n + 4$ b) 259

Page 63:
a) Yes, n = 83 b) No, n = 23.33 c) Yes, n = 90 d) No, n = 29.5 e) No, n = 41.09 f) Yes, n = 74
g) No, n = 45.77 h) No, n = 41.32 i) Yes, n = 46 j) No, n = 89.11

Page 64:
Red: A) (2, 1) B) (6, 3) C) (10, 11) D) (9, 9) E) (8, 4) F) (4, 12) G) (1, 9.5) H) (5.5, 8)
I) (11, 5.5) J) (3.5, 6)
Orange: A) (-5, 5) B) (5, 6) C) (-3, 2) D) (0, 0) E) (-3, -4) F) (4, -1) G) (4.5, -5.5)
H) (-1.5, 5.5) I) (3, 3) J) (2.5, -5.5)
a) (2, 5) b) (5, 1) c) (11, 11) d) (5, 2.5) e) (7.5, 5.5) f) (2.5, 15.5) g) (-3, 3) h) (-3, -3)
i) (-6, -3) j) (-7, -9) k) (-1.5, 2.5) l) (4.5, -6.5) m) (-4.5, -1.5) n) (-7.5, 6.5)
Exam question: (5x, 4y)

Page 65:
a) $y = 4$ b) $x = 2$ c) $x = 4$ d) $y = 1$ e) $x = -4$ f) $y = -2$ g) $y = 0$ h) $x = -1$ i) $x = -2.5$ j) $y = -5$ k) $x = 0$
l) $y = 1.5$

Solutions

Page 66:

a) 4 b) 1 c) 0 d) 7 e) 2 f) 3 g) 0 h) 1 i) -4 j) -1 k) -3 l) -2

Exam question: 4

Page 67:

a) 2 b) 1 c) 3 d) -1 e) 3 f) 2 g) 1 h) 4 i) -2 j) -3 k) -1 l) -6

Exam question: 2

Page 68:

a) $y = 2x$ b) $y = x + 1$ c) $y = -x + 7$ d) $y = -2x + 8$ e) $y = 2x - 1$ f) $y = x - 3$ g) $y = 5x + 2$ h) $y = 3x + 6$
i) $y = -x - 1$ j) $y = -1.5x - 2$ k) $y = -3x - 4$ l) $y = -2x - 1$

Exam question: $y = 4x - 3$

Page 69:

a) 7, (0, 2) b) 5, (0, 4) c) $\frac{1}{2}$, (0, -6) d) 1, (0, 9) e) 3, (0, 0) f) -4, (0, 7) g) -8, (0, -1) h) -3, (0, 9)
i) -1, (0, -11) j) $y = 4x + 3$ k) $y = 8x + 9$ l) $y = -2x + 6$ m) $y = x - 7$ n) $y = 9x - 3$ o) $y = -6x - 4$
p) $y = -x + 6$ q) $y = 3x$

Page 70:

a) (-1, 3), (0, 4), (1, 5), (2, 6)
b) (-1, -2), (0, 0), (1, 2), (2, 4)
c) (0, -3), (1, -2), (2, -1), (3, 0)
d) (-2, -3), (-1, -1), (0, 1), (1, 3)
e) (-1, -4), (0, -2), (1, 0), (2, 2)
f) (1, 4), (2, 3), (3, 2), (4, 1)

Exam question: -11, -7, -3, 1, 5

Page 71:

a)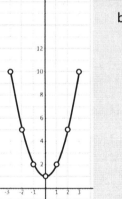

b)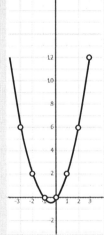

c)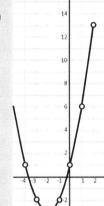

d)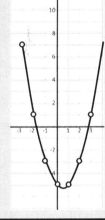

139

Page 72:

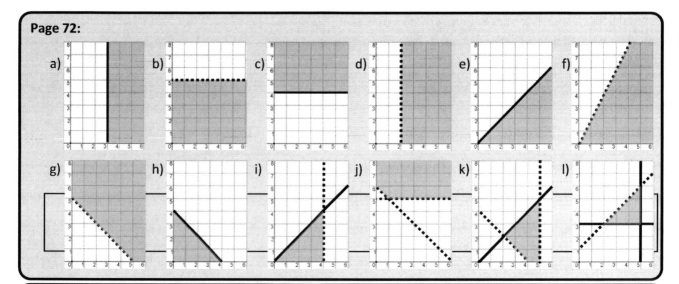

Page 73:

a) ₱1000 b) ₱250 c) £20 d) £12 e) ₱450 f) £30 g) £22 h) ₱850 i) £28/£29 j) $56 k) $7 l) £32
m) $21 n) £36 o) $70 p) £71/£72 q) Approximately ₱350 r) Approximately $22

Exam question: a) 140 fluid ounces b) 1.7 Litres

Page 74:

a) 120° – corresponding angles are equal b) 50° – vertically opposite angles are equal
c) 45° – alternate angles are equal d) 60° – corresponding angles are equal
e) 140° – vertically opposite angles are equal f) 113° – co-interior angles sum to 180°
g) 85° – alternate angles are equal h) 85° – co-interior angles sum to 180°
i) 115° – alternate angles are equal j) 100° – co-interior angles sum to 180°
k) 142° – alternate angles are equal l) 61° – corresponding angles are equal

Exam question: x = 70° because 78 + 32 + x = 180 as co-interior angles sum to 180°   or
x = 70° because angle ACB - 32 because alternate angles are equal then angles in a triangle sum to 180°

Page 75:

a) 105° b) 85° c) 120° d) 135° e) 55° f) 11° g) 109.5° h) 111.5° i) 127.7° j) Int = 60°, Ext = 120°
k) Int = 90°, Ext = 90° l) Int = 108°, Ext = 72° m) Int = 128.6°, Ext = 51.4° n) Int = 144°, Ext = 36°
o) Int = 135°, Ext = 45° p) Int = 120°, Ext = 60°   q) Int = 160°, Ext = 20°

Exam question: 12 sides

Page 76:

a) 180° b) 360° c) 540° d) 900° e) 720° f) 1080° g) 2340° h) 18000° i) 108° j) 144° k) 140°
l) 128.6° m) 171° n) 150° o) 175° p) 176.6°

Exam question: 147.3°

Page 77:

a) 156° b) 124° c) 35° d) 200° e) 109°

Exam question: $x + 2x + 96 + 144 + 102 = 540$ → $3x + 342 = 540$ → $x = 66$ so angle CDE = 132°

Page 78:

a) 040° b) 112°   c) 095°   d) 135°   e) 305°   f) 260°   g) 250° h) 060°
i) 050° j) 130°   k) 95°   l) 090°
Exam question: $180 - 60 = 120°$ $360 - 120 = 240°$

Page 79:
a) 6m/s b) 6km/h c) 8mph d) 8m/s e) 3km/h f) 27m g) 500 miles h) 276km i) 187200m
j) 0.422km k) 22s l) 18s m) 8 hours n) 200s o) 0.3 hours or 18 minutes

Exam question: 5400km

Page 80:
a) $3g/cm^3$ b) $8kg/m^3$ c) $9g/cm^3$ d) $15g/cm^3$ e) $2kg/m^3$ f) 16g g) 96kg h) 270g i) 640g j) 44.8kg
k) $4cm^3$ l) $7.5cm^3$ m) $10.7m^3$ n) $0.3m^3$ o) $5000cm^3$

Exam question: 1083g

Page 81:
a) 5Pa b) 17Pa c) 6.125Pa d) 22.5Pa e) 500Pa f) 112N g) 1400N h) 1320N i) 2.4N j) 0.1N k) $3m^3$
l) $2.7m^2$ m) $12.5m^2$ n) $4m^2$ o) $255m^2$

Exam question: 5.25Pa

Page 82:
a) A: Moving away at a constant speed, B: Moving back at a constant speed
b) A: Moving away at a constant speed, B: Stationary, C: Moving back at a constant speed
c) A: Moving away at a constant speed, B: Stationary, C: Moving away at a constant speed (faster than A)
d) A and B: Stationary, C: Moving back at a constant speed
e) A: Moving away (accelerating)
f) A: Stationary, B: Moving back at a constant speed, C: Moving back (decelerating)

Exam question: E, D, C, A, B

Page 83:
a) 1.2km/h b) 4m/s c) A: 2mph, B: 2mph d) A: 14km/h, B: 7km/h e) A: 7.5m/s, B: 2.5m/s
f) A: 2.8mph, B: 8mph, C: 1.067mph g) 8km/h h) 2.727m/s i) 2.036mph

Exam question: a) 20km/h b) 1.5 hours (1 hour 30 mins) c) 10km/h

---

Page 84:
a) A: Constant acceleration b) A: Constant velocity c) A: Constant deceleration
d) A: Constant acceleration B: Constant deceleration
e) A: Constant acceleration B: Constant velocity C: Constant deceleration
f) A: Constant acceleration B: Constant velocity C: Constant acceleration (faster than A)
g) A and B: Constant velocity C: Constant deceleration h) A: Non-constant acceleration
i) A: Constant velocity B: Constant deceleration c) Non-constant deceleration

---

Page 85:
a)   b) 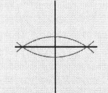 c)   d)

Page 86:
a) 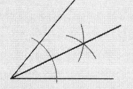 b) 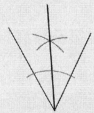 c) 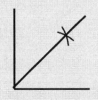 d)

Solutions

Page 87:
Approximately....
a) 640m b) 392m c) 256m d) 192m
e) 800m f) 584m g) 832m h) 440m

i) 2.5cm north of the windmill
j) 1cm south of the lagoon
k) 5.5cm west of mine
l) 3.75cm south east of the cabin

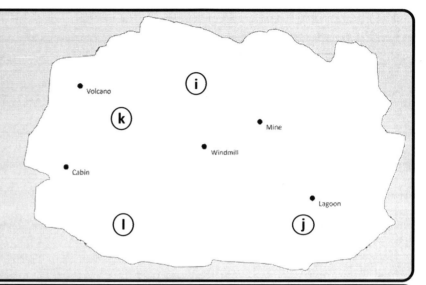

Page 88:
a) 15.71cm b) 37.70cm c) 9.42m d) 43.98mm e) 75.40cm f) 30.79mm g) 25.13cm h) 56.55cm
i) 106.81mm j) 30.16cm k) 43.04mm l) 540.35cm m) 33.42m n) 164.53mm o) 66.84m
Exam question: 1.88m

Page 89:
a) 50.27cm² b) 254.47cm² c) 907.92mm² d) 72.38cm² e) 339.79m² f) 23235.22cm² g) 19.63cm²
h) 113.10cm² i) 7.07m² j) 153.94mm² k) 452.39cm² l) 75.43mm² m) 25π cm² n) 64π cm² o) 36π cm²
Exam question: 40.7m²

Page 90:
a) 90° b) 90° c) 7cm d) 90° e) 8cm f) 32° g) 12cm h) 47° i) 63° j)129° k) 56° l) 237° m) 332°
n) 68° o) 57.5°
Exam question: $\angle ABO = \angle ACO = 90°$
$\angle BOC = 360 - (90 + 90 + 50) = 130°$

Page 91:
a) 5cm b) 37cm c) 26cm d) 13cm e) 20.62cm f) 47.85cm g) 9.48cm h) 89.63cm i) 15.62mm
Exam question: 16.97 miles

Page 92:
a) 12cm b) 21cm c) 45cm d) 14.66cm e) 15.33cm f) 9.64cm g) 35.71m h) 29.93cm i) 61.48cm
Exam question: 250 feet

Page 93:
a) Adjacent b) Hypotenuse c) Opposite d) Adjacent e) Adjacent f) Hypotenuse g) Opposite
h) Adjacent i) Sin j) Cos k) Tan l) Sin m) Cos n) Tan o) Sin p) Tan

Page 94:
a) 5cm b) 5.43 c) 20m d) 39.39mm e) 47.46cm f) 9.23cm g) 34.90.cm h) 11.04m i) 38.74cm
j) 124.20m
Exam question: 3.5m

Page 95:
a) 36.03° b) 36.87° c) 38.68° d) 55.15° e) 60.95° f) 56.44° g) 60.07° h) 40.60° i) 55.95° j) 30.67°
Exam question: 24.8°

Page 96:
a) 051° b) 132° c) 288° d) 246°

Page 97:
Set 1: a) 600cm b) 90mm c) 5000m d) 410cm e) 7cm f) 2m g) 2.4km h) 0.06m i) 2.4mm
j) 7000cm k) 6.4cm l) 60000cm
Set 2: a) 3000g b) 8000mg c) 12000kg d) 7.3T e) 4g f) 0.9T g) 0.65kg h) 0.065T i) 31000000g
j) 92000kg k) 720000000mg l) 630000mg
Set 3: a) 9000ml b) 50ml c) 5400ml d) 9400cl e) 80cl f) 3L g) 940cl h) 75L i) 22L j) 6500ml
k) 0.36L l) 2540ml
Exam question: 5.7kg

Page 98:
a) $110000cm^2$ b) $700mm^2$ c) $8000000m^2$ d) $60000cm^2$ e) $0.9cm^2$ f) $0.006m^2$ g) $0.0009km^2$ h) $0.08m^2$
i) $5000mm^2$ j) $4200000cm^2$ k) $0.64cm^3$ l) $5000000000cm^2$ m) $13000000cm^2$ n) $7000mm^3$
o) $8000000000m^3$ p) $5600000cm^3$ q) $0.03cm^3$ r) $0.0006m^3$ s) $0.000005km^3$ t) $0.0004m^3$ u) $70000mm^3$
v) $500000000cm^3$ w) $0.082cm^3$ x) $900000000000000cm^3$ y) $0.084L$ z) $4000cm^3$ α) $0.6L$ β) $50000cm^3$
γ) $900000L$ δ) $0.0047m^3$ ε) $0.0008L$ μ) $60000000mm^3$

Page 99:
a) 8.33m/s b) 20m/s c) 144km/h d) 55.56m/s e) 172.8km/h f) 21.24km/h g) 1.62m/s h) 1152km/h
i) 23.53m/s

Page 100:
a) $24cm^2$ b) $150cm^2$ c) $216cm^2$ d) $294cm^2$ e) $864cm^2$ f) $0.24m^2$ g) $62cm^2$ h) $126cm^2$ i) $52cm^2$
j) $130cm^2$ k) $180cm^2$ l) $240cm^2$
Exam question: $136cm^2$

Page 101:
a) $6cm^3$ b) $9cm^3$ c) $9cm^3$ d) $10cm^3$ e) $12cm^3$ f) $8cm^3$ g) $12cm^3$ h) $24cm^3$ i) $36cm^3$ j) $24cm^3$
k) $90cm^3$ l) $30cm^3$ m) $100cm^3$ n) $120m^3$ o) $144mm^3$
Exam question: $96cm^3$

Page 102:
a) $70cm^3$ b) $72m^3$ c) $240cm^3$ d) $45cm^3$ e) $112.5cm^3$ f) $180cm^3$ g) $198cm^3$ h) $628m^3$ i) $471cm^3$
j) $308m^3$ k) $402cm^3$ l) $62.8m^3$
Exam question: 20p

Page 103:
a) $60m^2$ b) $111.6m^2$ c) $174.4m^2$ d) $311.9cm^2$ e) $288.1cm^2$ f) $215cm^2$ g) $111.6m^2$ h) $156.9m^2$
Exam question: £528.68

Page 104:
a) $345.6cm^2$ b) $207.4cm^2$ c) $326.7cm^2$ d) $188.5cm^2$ e) $88.0m^2$ f) $301.6cm^2$ g) $377.0cm^2$
h) $252.9m^2$ i) $460.6cm^2$ j) $181mm^2$
Exam question: 90π cm^2

Page 105:
a) 8cm b) 70° c) 21cm d) 6cm e) 44° f) 6cm g) 21cm h) 19.2cm i) 16cm
Exam question: 3.75cm

Page 106:

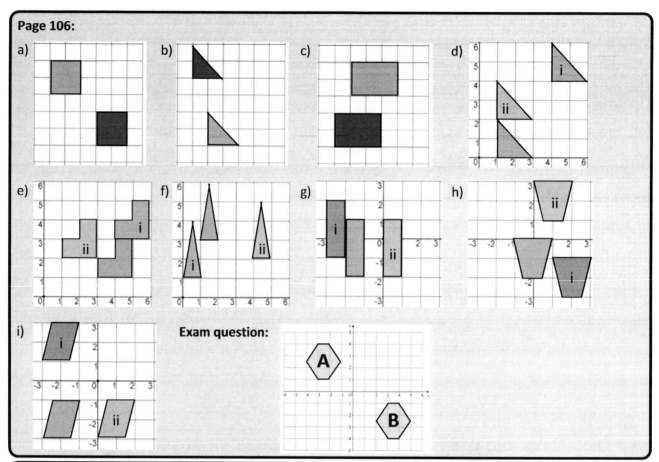

a) b) c) d)

e) f) g) h)

i) **Exam question:**

Page 107:

a) Translation by the vector $\begin{pmatrix} 3 \\ 2 \end{pmatrix}$ b) Translation by the vector $\begin{pmatrix} 1 \\ 3 \end{pmatrix}$ c) Translation by the vector $\begin{pmatrix} 5 \\ 1 \end{pmatrix}$

d) Translation by the vector $\begin{pmatrix} -1 \\ 4 \end{pmatrix}$ e) Translation by the vector $\begin{pmatrix} 3 \\ 4 \end{pmatrix}$ f) Translation by the vector $\begin{pmatrix} 2 \\ 0 \end{pmatrix}$

g) Translation by the vector $\begin{pmatrix} -3 \\ -1 \end{pmatrix}$ h) Translation by the vector $\begin{pmatrix} 0 \\ -3 \end{pmatrix}$ i) Translation by the vector $\begin{pmatrix} -3 \\ 2 \end{pmatrix}$

Exam question: Translation by the vector $\begin{pmatrix} -6 \\ 2 \end{pmatrix}$

Page 108:

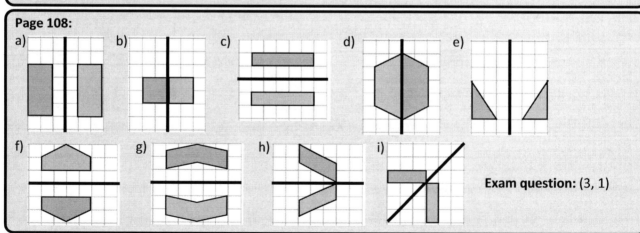

a) b) c) d) e)

f) g) h) i) **Exam question:** (3, 1)

Solutions

Page 109:

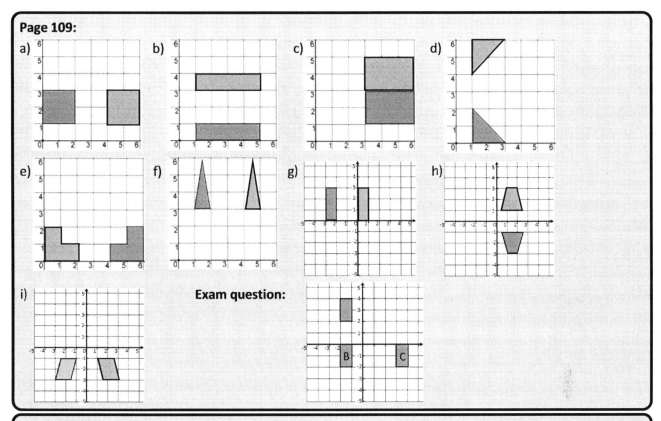

a)

b)

c)

d)

e)

f)

g)

h)

i)

Exam question:

Page 110:
a) Reflection in the line y = 3   b) Reflection in the line x = 3   c) Reflection in the line y = 2.5
d) Reflection in the line x = 2   e) Reflection in the line y = 4   f) Reflection in the line x = 2.5
g) A to B: Reflection in the line x = -1.5,   A to C: Reflection in the line y = 0 (or x-axis)
h) A to B: Reflection in the line x = -1,   A to C: Reflection in the line y = 0.5
i) A to B: Reflection in the line y = x,   A to C: Reflection in the line y = -1

Exam question: Reflection in the line x = -1

Page 111:
a)

b)

c)

d)

e)

f)

g)

h)

i)

Exam question:

Page 112:
a) Rotation, 90° clockwise about the point (1, 2) b) Rotation, 90° anti-clockwise about the point (5, 3)
c) Rotation, 180° about the point (3, 3) d) Rotation, 180° about the point (3, 2)
e) Rotation, 90° clockwise about the point (4, 4) f) Rotation, 90° anti-clockwise about the point (4, 3)
g) Rotation, 90° anti-clockwise about the point (1, 1) h) Rotation, 180° about the point (0, 0)

Exam question: Rotation, 90° anti-clockwise about the point (1, 1)

Page 113:
a) 2 b) 5 c) 4 d) 7 e) 8 f) 0.5 g) 0.25 h) 1.5

Exam question: 16cm

Page 114:

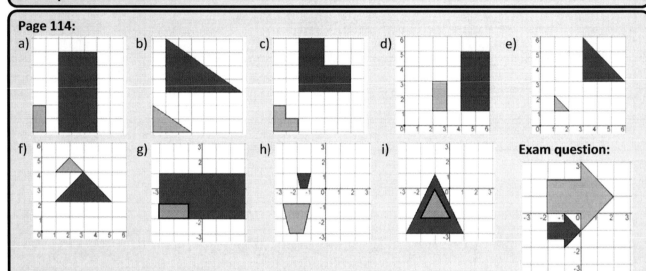

Page 115:
a) (1, 1) b) (4, 0) c) (0, 3) d) (0, 1) e) (3.5, 0) f) (0, 0) g) (-4, -1) h) (-3, 0) i) (1, 0)

Exam question: (2, 1)

Page 116:
a) 32 b) 160 c) 70 d) 3 e) 18 f) 19 g) 15 h) 10 i) 21

Exam question: 2.5 stars

Page 117:
a) i) 45 ii) 33 iii) 78 iv) 9.75 b) 11.533 c) 1.627m d) 5.706kg

Exam question: 3 hours 45 mins

Page 118:
a) i) 438 ii) 1120 iii) 682 iv) 17.05 b) 36.8 c) 1.788 d) 4.083

Exam question: 150 minutes or 2.5 hours

Page 119:
a) Mode: 0 Median: 1 b) Mode: 6 Median: 6 c) Mode: 15 Median: 14 d) Mode: 2 Median: 2

Exam question: a) 32 b) 31

Page 120:
a) 1 b) 6 c) 13.6 d) 2.34   **Exam question:** 30.35

Page 121:

a) Modal class: $0 \leq x < 2$ Median class: $0 \leq x < 2$ b) Modal class: $7 \leq x < 9$ Median class: $5 \leq x < 7$

c) Modal class: $20 \leq x < 30$ Median class: $20 \leq x < 30$ d) Modal class: $18 \leq x < 24$ Median class: $12 \leq x < 18$

Exam question: a) $0 < m \leq 10$ b) $10 < m \leq 20$

Page 122:

a) 2 b) 6 c) 27.105 d) 15.364   **Exam question:** 28.25 minutes

---

Page 123:

a) 0.4 b) 0.9 c) 0.42 d) 0.19 e) 0.575 f) 0.363 g) 0.108 h) 0.972 i) $\frac{1}{2}$ j) $\frac{3}{7}$ k) $\frac{5}{13}$ l) $\frac{16}{21}$ m) $\frac{12}{17}$ n) $\frac{41}{77}$

o) $\frac{110}{123}$ p) $\frac{183}{241}$ q) 0.6 r) 0 s) $\frac{6}{11}$ t) 0.03 u) 0.23 v) $\frac{34}{99}$ w) 0.165 x) 0.122 y) $\frac{124}{873}$ z) x = 0.1

Exam question: White: 0.15, Blue: 0.15

Page 124:

a) $\frac{2}{10}$ b) $\frac{3}{10}$ c) $\frac{4}{10}$ d) $\frac{8}{10}$ e) $\frac{5}{10}$ f) $\frac{5}{10}$ g) $\frac{2}{10}$ h) $\frac{3}{10}$ i) $\frac{7}{10}$ j) $\frac{8}{11}$ k) $\frac{3}{11}$ l) $\frac{4}{11}$ m) $\frac{4}{11}$ n) $\frac{8}{11}$ o) $\frac{7}{11}$

p) $\frac{2}{6}$ q) $\frac{3}{6}$ r) $\frac{6}{6}$ or 1 s) $\frac{4}{6}$ t) $\frac{3}{6}$ u) $\frac{2}{6}$ **Exam question:** a) $\frac{4}{7}$ b) $\frac{2}{7}$

Page 125:

a) $\frac{1}{100}$ b) $\frac{2}{100}$ c) $\frac{4}{100}$ d) $\frac{12}{100}$ e) $\frac{4}{100}$ f) $\frac{6}{100}$ g) 0.42 h) 0.12 i) 0.28 j) 0.18 k) 0.46 l) 0.88

Exam question: a) $\frac{9}{42}$ b) $\frac{40}{42}$

Page 126:

a)
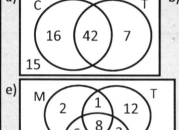

b)
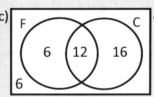

c)
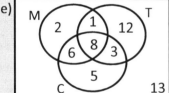

d)
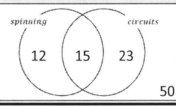

e)
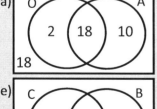

Exam question:
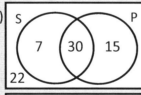

Page 127:

a)
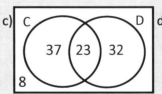

b)

c)

d)
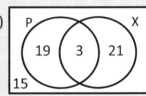

e)
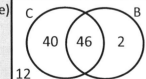

f)
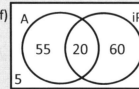

Exam question:
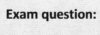
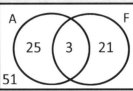

Page 128:

a) {3, 5} b) {3, 9} c) {1, 2, 3, 4, 5, 6, 7, 10} d) {1, 7} e) {2, 3, 4, 5, 6, 8, 9, 10} f) {10} g) {1, 2, 4, 6, 7, 8, 10}

h) {2, 4, 10} i) {1, 2, 3, 4, 5, 6, 7} j) {1, 7} k) {1, 2, 4, 7} l) {1, 2, 3, 4, 5, 6, 7, 8, 9}

m) $\frac{2}{10}$ n) $\frac{8}{10}$ o) $\frac{2}{10}$ p) $\frac{7}{10}$ q) $\frac{3}{10}$ r) $\frac{8}{10}$ **Exam question:** a) $\frac{7}{16}$ b) {1, 2, 4, 7, 8, 11, 13, 14, 16}

Page 129:

a) 5 b) 3 c) 3 d) 1 e) 4 f) 8 g) 9 h) 8 i) True j) False k) False l) True m) True n) True o) True

p) False q) True r) False s) True t) False u) True v) True w) True

Page 130:

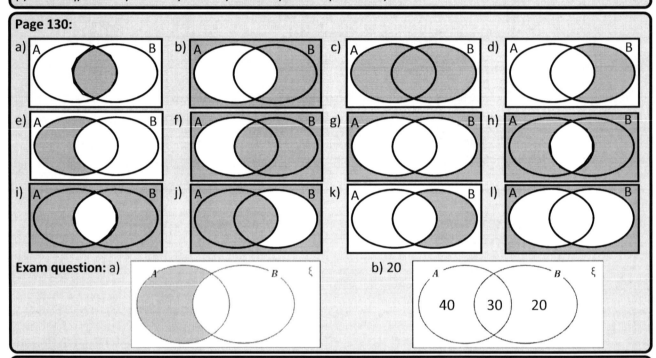

Exam question: a)

b) 20

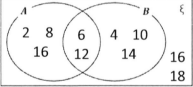

Page 131:

a) $\frac{4}{7}$ b) $\frac{2}{7}$ c) $\frac{3}{7}$ d) $\frac{1}{7}$ e) $\frac{5}{7}$ f) $\frac{5}{7}$ g) $\frac{5}{10}$ h) $\frac{2}{10}$ i) $\frac{7}{10}$ j) $\frac{2}{10}$ k) $\frac{3}{10}$ l) $\frac{3}{10}$ m) $\frac{5}{12}$ n) $\frac{9}{12}$ o) $\frac{7}{12}$ p) $\frac{3}{12}$ q) $\frac{3}{12}$ r) $\frac{11}{12}$

s) $\frac{1}{11}$ t) $\frac{3}{11}$ u) $\frac{9}{11}$ v) $\frac{10}{11}$ w) $\frac{2}{11}$ x) $\frac{9}{11}$

Exam question: a)

A: 2 8 16
A∩B: 6 12
B: 4 10 14
16
18

b) $\frac{8}{10}$

Printed in Great Britain
by Amazon